History of the United States

History
of the
United States

from the
Earliest Discovery of America
to the Present time

By

E. Benjamin Andrews

Volume 1

Ross & Perry, Inc.
Washington, D.C.

Copyright 1804, Charles Scribner's Sons
Reprinted by Ross & Perry, Inc. 2002
© Ross & Perry, Inc. 2002 on new material. All rights reserved.

Protected under the Berne Convention.

Printed in The United States of America

Ross & Perry, Inc. Publishers
216 G St., N.E.
Washington, D.C. 20002
Telephone (202) 675-8300
Facsimile (202) 675-8400
info@RossPerry.com

SAN 253-8555

Library of Congress Control Number: 2002105376
http://www.rossperry.com

ISBN 1-932080-16-3

Book Cover designed by Sapna. sapna@rossperry.com

⊗ The paper used in this publication meets the requirements for permanence
established by the American National Standard for Information Sciences
"Permanence of Paper for Printed Library Materials" (ANSI Z39.48-1984).

All rights reserved. No copyrighted part of this publication may be reproduced,
stored in a retrieval system, or transmitted, in any form or by any means,
electronic, photocopying, recording, or otherwise, without the prior written
permission of the publisher.

Columbus.

After a portrait by Herrera.

TO MY WIFE

PREFACE

NOTWITHSTANDING the number of United States histories already in existence, and the excellence of many of them, I venture to think that no apology is needed for bringing forward another.

1. The work now presented to the public is believed to utilize, more than any of its predecessors, the many valuable researches of recent years into the rich archives of this and other nations.

2. Most of the briefer treatments of the subject are manuals, intended for pupils in schools, the conspicuous articulation so necessary for this purpose greatly lessening their interest for the general reader. The following narrative will be found continuous as well as of moderate compass.

3. I have sought to make more prominent than popular histories have usually

done, at the same time the political evolution of our country on the one hand, and the social culture, habits, and life of the people on the other.

4. The work strives to observe scrupulous proportion in treating the different parts and phases of our national career, neglecting none and over-emphasizing none. Also, while pronouncedly national and patriotic, it is careful to be perfectly fair and kind to the people of all sections.

5. Effort has been made to present the matter in the most natural periods and divisions, and to give such a title to each of these as to render the table of contents a truthful and instructive epitome of our national past.

6. With the same aim the Fore-history is exhibited in sharp separation from the United States history proper, calling due attention to what is too commonly missed, the truly epochal character of the adoption of our present Constitution, in 1789.

7. Copious illustration has been employed, with diligent study to make it for

every reader in the highest degree an instrument of instruction, delight, and cultivation in art.

8. No pains has been spared to secure perfect accuracy in all references to dates, persons, and places, so that the volumes may be used with confidence as a work of reference. I am persuaded that much success in this has been attained, despite the uncertainty still attaching to many matters of this sort in United States history, especially to dates.

BROWN UNIVERSITY, September 15, 1894.

PUBLISHERS' NOTE

THE last edition of President Andrews's History was issued in 1905, in five volumes, and brought the narrative down to the inauguration of President Roosevelt in March of that year. In preparing the extension of the work by the addition of a sixth volume, entrusted to the competent hands of Professor James Alton James of Northwestern University, it has been thought desirable to begin this final volume with the chapters entitled "The Rise of Roosevelt" and "Mr. Roosevelt's Presidency." This has involved some expansion and revision of these chapters as well as the continuance of the History from 1905 to the present time. The Appendices, which include public documents of fundamental importance and the significant results in various fields of the Census of 1910, are an additional feature of the new edition.

CONTENTS

INTRODUCTION

AMERICA BEFORE COLUMBUS 21

Age and Origin of Man in America.—Primordial Americans unlike Present Asiatics.—Resemblances between their Various Branches.—Two Great Types.—The Mound-builders' Age.—Design of the Mounds.—Different Forms.—Towns and Cities.—Proofs of Culture.—Arts.—Fate of the Mound-builders.—The Indians.—Their Number.—Degree of Civilization.—Power of Endurance.—Religion.—The Various Nations.—Original Brute Inhabitants of North America.—Plants, Fruits, and Trees.—Indian Agriculture.

Part First
THE FORE-HISTORY

PERIOD I

DISCOVERY AND SETTLEMENT
1492–1660

CHAPTER I. COLUMBUS 37

Bretons and Normans in the New World.—The Northmen Question.—Marco Polo's Travels.—His Pictures of Eastern Asia.—Influence on Columbus.—Early Life of Columbus.—His Cruises and Studies.—Asia to be Reached by Sailing West.—

Appeals for Aid.—Rebuffs.—Success.—Sails from Palos.—The Voyage.—America Discovered.—Columbus's Later Voyages and Discoveries.—Illusion Respecting the New Land.—Amerigo Vespucci.—Rise of the Name "America."

                                                                PAGE
CHAPTER II. EARLY SPANISH AMERICA . . 62

Portugal and Spain Divide the Newly Discovered World.—Spain gets most of America.—Voyage of de Solis.—Balboa Discovers the Pacific.—Ponce de Leon on the Florida Coast.—Explorations by Grijalva.—Cortez Invades Mexico.—Subjugates the Country.—De Ayllon's Cruise.—Magellan Circumnavigates the Globe.—Narvaez's Expedition into Florida.—Its Sad Fate.—De Soto.—His March.—Hardships.—Discovers the Mississippi.—His Death.—End of his Expedition.—French Settlement in Florida.—St. Augustine.—French-Spanish Hostilities.—Reasons for Spain's Failure to Colonize far North.—Her Treatment of the Natives.—Tyranny over her own Colonies.

CHAPTER III. EXPLORATION AND COLONIZATION BY THE FRENCH AND THE ENGLISH . 93

Verrazano.—"New France."—Cartier Discovers St. Lawrence Gulf and River.—Second Voyage.—Montreal.—Third.—De Monts.—Champlain.—Founds Quebec.—Westward Explorations.—John Cabot, Discoverer of the North American Main.—Frobisher.—Tries for a Northwest Passage.—Second Expedition for Gold.—Third.—Eskimo Tradition of Frobisher's Visits.—Drake Sails round the World.—Cavendish Follows.—Raleigh's Scheme.—Colony at Roanoke Island.—"Virginia."—Second Colony.—Its Fate.

CHAPTER IV. THE PLANTING OF VIRGINIA . 114

The Old Virginia Charter.—Jamestown Settled.—Company and Colony.—Character of Early Virginia Population.—Progress.—Products.—Slavery.—Agriculture the Dominant Industry.—No Town Life.—Hardships and Dissensions.—John Smith.—New Charter.—Delaware Governor.—The "Starving Time."—

CONTENTS 11

Severe Rule of Dale and Argall.—The Change of 1612.—Pocahontas.—Indian Hostilities.—First American Legislature.—Sir Thomas Wyatt.—Self-Government.—Virginia Reflects English Political Progress.—Dissolution of the Company.—Charles I. and Virginia.—Harvey, Wyatt, Berkeley.—Virginia under Cromwell.

PAGE

CHAPTER V. PILGRIM AND PURITAN AT THE
  NORTH 131

The first "Independents."—John Smyth's Church at Gainsborough.—The Scrooby Church.—Plymouth Colony.—Settles Plymouth.—Hardships.—Growth.—Cape Ann Settlement.—Massachusetts Bay.—Size.—Polity.—Roger Williams.—His Views. —His Exile.—Anne Hutchinson.—Rhode Island Founded.— Settlement of Hartford, Windsor, Wethersfield.—Saybrook.— New Haven.—New Hampshire.—Maine.—New England Confederation.—Its Function.—Its Failure.

CHAPTER VI. BALTIMORE AND HIS MARYLAND 150

Sir George Calvert Plants at Newfoundland.—Is Ennobled.— Sails for Virginia.—Grant of Maryland.—Lord Baltimore Dies.— Succeeded by Cecil.—Government of Maryland.—Conflict with Virginia.—Baltimore comes to Maryland.—Religious Freedom in the Colony.—Clayborne's Rebellion.—First Maryland Assembly.—Anarchy.—Romanism Established.—Baltimore and Roger Williams.—Maryland during the Civil War in England.—Death of Baltimore.—Character.—Maryland under the Long Parliament. —Puritan Immigration.—Founds Annapolis.—Rebellion.—Clayborne again.—Maryland and the Commonwealth.—Deposition of Governor Stone.—Anti-Catholic Laws.—Baltimore Defied.— Sustained by Cromwell.—Fendall's Rebellion.—Fails.—Maryland at the Restoration.

CHAPTER VII. NEW NETHERLAND . . 265

Henry Hudson and his Explorations.—Enters Hudson River. —His Subsequent Career.—And his Fate.—Dutch Trade on the

CONTENTS

Hudson.—" New Netherland."—Dutch West India Company.—Albany Begun.—New Amsterdam.—Relations with Plymouth.—De Vries on the Delaware.—Dutch Fort at Hartford.—Conflict of Dutch with English.—Gustavus Adolphus.—Swedish Beginnings at Wilmington, Delaware.—Advent of Kieft.—Maltreats Indians. — New Netherland in 1647. — Stuyvesant's Excellent Rule.—Conquers New Sweden.—And the Indians.—Conquest of Dutch America by England.—" New York.'—Persistence of Dutch Influence and Traits.

PAGE
CHAPTER VIII. THE FIRST INDIAN WARS . 181

Beginning of Indian Hostility.—Of Pequot War.—Mason's Strategy.—And Tactics.—Capture of Pequot Fort.—Back to Saybrook.—Extermination of Pequot Tribe.—Peace.—Miantonomoh and Uncas.—Dutch War with Indians.—Caused by Kieft's Impolicy.—Liquor.—Underhill Comes.—Mrs. Hutchinson's Fate. Deborah Moody.—New Haven Refuses Aid.—Appeal to Holland. —Underhill's Exploits.—Kieft Removed.—Sad Plight of New Netherland.—Subsequent Hostilities and Final Peace.

PERIOD II

ENGLISH AMERICA TILL THE END OF THE FRENCH AND INDIAN WAR

1660-1763

CHAPTER I. NEW ENGLAND UNDER THE LAST
    STUARTS 201

Charles II. and Massachusetts.—Massachusetts about 1660.—Its View of its Political Rights.—The King's View.—And Commands.—Commission of 1664.—Why Vengeance was Delayed.—Boldness of the Colony.—It Buys Maine.—Fails to get New Hampshire.—The King's Rage.—The Charter Vacated.—Charles II. and Connecticut.—Prosperity of this Colony.—Rhode Island. —Boundary Disputes of Connecticut.—Of Rhode Island.—

CONTENTS

George Fox and Roger Williams.—James II. King.—Andros Governor.—Andros and Southern New England.—In Massachusetts.—Revolution of 1688.—New Charter for Massachusetts.—Defects and Merits.

PAGE

CHAPTER II. KING PHILIP'S WAR . . . 220

Whites' Treatment of Red Men.—Indian Hatred.—Causes.—Alexander's Death.—Philip King.—Scope of his Conspiracy.—Murders Sausaman.—War Begun.—Nipmucks take Part.—War in Connecticut Valley.—Bloody Brook.—The Swamp Fight at South Kingston, R. I.—Central Massachusetts Aflame.—The Rowlandson History.—Southeastern Massachusetts and Rhode Island again.—Connecticut Valley once more Invaded.—Turner's Falls.—Philip's Death.—Horrors of the War.—Philip's Character.—Fate of his Family.

CHAPTER III. THE SALEM WITCHCRAFT . 237

New England Home Life.—Religion its Centre.—The Farmhouse.—Morning Devotions.—Farm Work.—Tools.—Diet.—Neighborliness.—New England Superstitions.—Not Peculiar to New England.—Sunday Laws.—Public Worship.—First Case of Sorcery.—The Witch Executed.—Cotton Mather.—His Experiments.—His Book.—The Parris Children Bewitched.—The Manifestations.—The Trial.—Executions.—George Burroughs.—Rebecca Nurse.—Reaction.—Forwardness of Clergy.—"Devil's Authority."—The End.

CHAPTER IV. THE MIDDLE COLONIES . . 257

English Conquest of New Netherland.—Duke of York's Government.—Andros.—Revolution of 1688.—Leisler.—Problems which Teased Royal Governors.—New Jersey.—Its Political Vicissitudes.—William Penn.—Character.—Liberality of Pennsylvania Charter.—Penn and James II.—Penn's Services for his Colony.—Prosperity of the Latter.—Fletcher's Rule.—Gabriel Thomas's History of Pennsylvania.—Penn's Trials.—And Victory.—Delaware.

CONTENTS

PAGE

CHAPTER V. MARYLAND, VIRGINIA, CAROLINA 273

Maryland after the Stuart Restoration.—Navigation Act.—Boundary Disputes.—Liberality of Religion.—Agitation to Establish Anglicanism.—Maryland under William and Mary.—English Church Established.—Not Oppressive.—Fate of Virginia after the Restoration.—Virginia's Spirit, Numbers, Resources.—Causes of Bacon's Rebellion.—Evil of the Navigation Acts.—Worthless Officials.—Course of the Rebellion.—Result.—Dulness of the Subsequent History.—William and Mary College.—Governor Spotswood.—Blackbeard.—Carolina.—Its Constitution.—Conflict of Parties.—Georgia.

CHAPTER VI. GOVERNMENTAL INSTITUTIONS IN THE COLONIES 293

Origin of American Political Institutions.—Local Self-Government.—Representation.—Relation of Colonies to England.—Classification of Colonies.—Changes.—Conflict of Legal Views.—Colonists' Contentions.—Taxation.

CHAPTER VII. SOCIAL CULTURE IN COLONIAL TIMES 299

Population of the Colonies at Different Dates.—Differences according to Sections.—Intellectual Ability.—Free Thought.—Political Bent.—English Church in the Colonies.—Its Clergy.—In New York.—The New England Establishment.—Hatred to Episcopacy.—Counter-hatred.—Colleges and Schools.—Newspapers.—Libraries.—Postal System.—Learned Professions.—Epidemics.—Scholars and Artists.—Travelling.—Manufactures and Commerce.—Houses.—Food and Dress.—Wigs.—Opposition to Them.—Social Cleavage.—Redemptioners.—Penal Legislation.—Philadelphia Leads in Social Science.

CHAPTER VIII. ENGLAND AND FRANCE IN AMERICA 323

The French in the Heart of the Continent.—Groseilliers. Radisson. La Salle.—Joliet and Marquette Reach the Mississippi

—Baudin and Du Lhut.—La Salle Descends to the Gulf.—" Chicago."—The Portages.—La Salle's Expedition from France to the Mississippi.—Its Fate.—French, Indians, and English.—France's Advantage.—Numbers of each Race in America.—Causes of England's Colonial Strength.—King William's War.—The Schenectady Massacre.—Other Atrocities.—Anne's War.—Deerfield.—Plans for Striking Back.—Second Capture of Port Royal.—Rasle's Settlement Raided.—George's War.—Capture of Louisburg.—Saratoga Destroyed.—Scheme to Retaliate.—Failure.—French Vigilance and Aggression.

CHAPTER IX. THE FRENCH AND INDIAN WAR 349

Struggle Inevitable.—George Washington.—Fights at Great Meadows.—War Begun.—English Plans of Campaign.—Braddock's March.—Defeat and Death.—Prophecy Regarding Washington.—The " Evangeline " History.—Loudon's Incompetence.—Pitt at the Head of Affairs.—Will Take Canada.—Louisburg Recaptured.—" Pittsburgh."—Triple Movement upon Canada.—The Plains of Abraham.—Quebec Capitulates.—Peace of Paris.—Conspiracy of Pontiac.

LIST OF ILLUSTRATIONS

	PAGE
COLUMBUS. (After a portrait by Herrera),	*Frontispiece*
TEMPLE MOUND IN MEXICO,	23
BIG ELEPHANT MOUND, WISCONSIN,	25
DIGHTON ROCK,	39
THE OLD STONE MILL AT NEWPORT, R. I.,	40
PRINCE HENRY OF PORTUGAL—"THE NAVIGATOR." (From an old print),	45
QUEEN ISABELLA OF SPAIN,	48
COLUMBUS BEGGING AT THE FRANCISCAN CONVENT,	50
EMBARKATION OF CHRISTOPHER COLUMBUS AT PALOS. (From an old print),	53
AMERIGO VESPUCCI. (Fac-simile of an old print),	59
VASCO DA GAMA. (From an old print),	63
BALBOA DISCOVERING THE PACIFIC OCEAN,	67
PONCE DE LEON,	69
HERNANDO CORTÈS. (From an old print),	71
MONTEZUMA MORTALLY WOUNDED BY HIS OWN SUBJECTS,	75
DEATH OF MAGELLAN,	79
FERDINAND DE SOTO,	81
A PALISADED INDIAN TOWN IN ALABAMA,	83
BURIAL OF DE SOTO IN THE MISSISSIPPI AT NIGHT,	85
FORT CAROLINA ON THE RIVER OF MAY,	86
PEDRO MELENDEZ,	87
INDIANS DEVOURED BY DOGS. (From an old print),	89
VERRAZANO, THE FLORENTINE NAVIGATOR,	94
JACQUES CARTIER. (From an old print),	95
SEBASTIAN CABOT. (From an old print),	101
AN INDIAN VILLAGE AT THE ROANOKE SETTLEMENT,	106
SIR HUMPHREY GILBERT,	108
SIR WALTER RALEIGH,	109

LIST OF ILLUSTRATIONS

	PAGE
QUEEN ELIZABETH,	112
KING JAMES I. (From Mr. Henry Irving's Collection),	115
TOBACCO PLANT,	119
CAPTAIN JOHN SMITH,	120
POCAHONTAS SAVING CAPTAIN SMITH'S LIFE. (From Smith's "General History"),	122
THE COUNCIL OF POWHATAN. (From Smith's "General History"),	125
POCAHONTAS,	127
SIGNATURE OF BERKELEY,	130
PLYMOUTH HARBOR, ENGLAND,	132
HARBOR OF PROVINCETOWN, CAPE COD, WHERE THE PILGRIMS LANDED,	133
THE LIFE OF THE COLONY AT CAPE COD,	134
SIGNATURES TO PLYMOUTH PATENT,	136
SITE OF FIRST CHURCH AND GOVERNOR BRADFORD'S HOUSE AT PLYMOUTH,	137
GOVERNOR WINTHROP,	139
FIRST CHURCH IN SALEM,	140
SEAL OF MASSACHUSETTS BAY COMPANY,	141
ROGER WILLIAMS' HOUSE AT SALEM,	143
EDWARD WINSLOW,	144
MARYLAND SHILLING,	150
HENRIETTA MARIA,	152
SUPPOSED PORTRAIT OF WILLIAM CLAYBORNE,	154
CLAYBORNE'S TRADING POST ON KENT ISLAND,	155
FIGHT BETWEEN CLAYBORNE AND THE ST. MARY'S SHIP,	157
OLIVER CROMWELL,	161
SEAL OF NEW AMSTERDAM,	166
PETER STUYVESANT,	167
SEAL OF NEW NETHERLAND,	169
EARLIEST PICTURE OF NEW AMSTERDAM,	171
DE VRIES,	172
COSTUMES OF SWEDES,	173
THE OLD STADT HUYS AT NEW AMSTERDAM,	176
NEW AMSTERDAM IN THE MIDDLE OF THE SEVENTEENTH CENTURY,	177
THE DUKE OF YORK, AFTERWARDS JAMES II.,	178
THE TOMB OF STUYVESANT,	179

LIST OF ILLUSTRATIONS

PAGE

ATTACK ON THE FORT OF THE PEQUOTS ON THE MYSTIC RIVER,	184, 185
ATTACK ON THE PEQUOT FORT,	188
SIGNATURE OF MIANTONOMOH,	191
THE GRAVE OF MIANTONOMOH,	193
TOTEM OR TRIBE MARK OF THE FIVE NATIONS,	199
KING CHARLES II.,	203
JOHN WINTHROP THE YOUNGER,	210
SIR EDMOND ANDROS,	214
THE CHARTER OAK AT HARTFORD,	216
BOX IN WHICH THE CONNECTICUT CHARTER WAS KEPT,	219
THE MONUMENT AT BLOODY BROOK,	227
GOFFE AT HADLEY,	229
INCREASE MATHER,	244
COTTON MATHER,	246
OLD TITUBA THE INDIAN,	248
LIEUTENANT-GOVERNOR STOUGHTON,	250
FAC-SIMILE OF SHERIFF'S RETURN OF AN EXECUTION,	252
SLOUGHTER SIGNING LEISLER'S DEATH WARRANT,	260
SEAL OF THE CARTERETS,	262
SEAL OF EAST JERSEY,	263
WAMPUM RECEIVED BY PENN IN COMMEMORATION OF THE INDIAN TREATY,	264
WILLIAM PENN,	265
THE TREATY MONUMENT, KENSINGTON,	268
THE PENN MANSION IN PHILADELPHIA,	270
CHARLES, SECOND LORD BALTIMORE,	274
REV. DR. BLAIR, FIRST PRESIDENT OF WILLIAM AND MARY COLLEGE,	281
GEORGE MONK, DUKE OF ALBEMARLE,	283
LORD SHAFTESBURY,	285
SEAL OF THE PROPRIETORS OF CAROLINA,	286
JOHN LOCKE,	287
SAVANNAH. (From a print of 1741),	289
JAMES OGLETHORPE,	291
COSTUMES ABOUT THE MIDDLE OF THE SEVENTEENTH CENTURY,	302, 303, 306, 307
JAMES LOGAN,	310
KING WILLIAM,	312

LIST OF ILLUSTRATIONS

	PAGE
Queen Mary,	313
Chief Justice Sewall,	319
The Pillory,	321
Signature of Jolliet (old spelling),	323
Totem of the Sioux,	323
A Sioux Chief,	324
Totem of the Illinois,	325
The Reception of Joliet and Marquette by the Illinois,	327
Louis XIV.,	331
Coins Struck in France for the Colonies,	332
Assassination of La Salle,	333
New Orleans in 1719,	334
Signature of D'Iberville,	335
The Attack on Schenectady,	337
Hannah Dustin's Escape,	339
Queen Anne,	343
Governor Shirley,	345
Sir William Pepperrell,	346
The Ambuscade,	351
The Death of Braddock,	357
Montcalm,	361
William Pitt,	362
General Wolfe,	364
Landing of Wolfe,	366
Quebec in 1730. (From an old print),	367
Bouquet's Redoubt at Pittsburgh,	369

LIST OF MAPS

Globus Martini Behaim Narinbergensis, 1492,	42
European Provinces in 1655,	*facing* 176
Marquette's Map,	330
Plan of Port Royal, Nova Scotia,	341
Map showing Position of French and English Forts and Settlements,	350
Braddock's Route,	354
Map of Braddock's Field,	356

INTRODUCTION

AMERICA BEFORE COLUMBUS

MAN made his appearance on the western continent unnumbered ages ago, not unlikely before the close of the glacial period. It is possible that human life began in Asia and western North America sooner than on either shore of the Atlantic. Nothing wholly forbids the belief that America was even the cradle of the race, or one of several cradles, though most scientific writers prefer the view that our species came hither from Asia. De Nadaillac judges it probable that the ocean was thus crossed not at Behring Strait alone, but along a belt of equatorial islands as well. We may think of successive waves of such immigration—perhaps the easiest way to account for certain differences among American races.

It is, at any rate, an error to speak of the primordial Americans as derived from any Asiatic stock at present existing or known to history. The old Americans had scarcely an Asiatic feature. Their habits and customs were emphatically peculiar to themselves. Those in which they agreed with the trans-Pacific populations, such as fashion of weapons and of fortifications, elements of folk-lore, religious ideas, traditions of a flood, belief in the destruction of the world by fire, and so on, are nearly all found the world over, the spontaneous creations of our common human intelligence.

The original American peoples, various and unlike as they were, agreed in four traits, three of them physical, one mental, which mark them off as in all likelihood primarily of one stock after all, and as different from any Old World men: (1) They had low, retreating foreheads. (2) Their hair was black. (3) It was also of a peculiar texture, lank, and cylindrical in section, never wavy. And (4) their languages were polysynthetic, forming a class apart from all others in the world. The peoples of America, if from Asia, must date back to a time when speech itself was in its infancy.

The numerous varieties of ancient Americans reduce to two distinct types

Temple Mound in Mexico.

—the Dolicocephalous or long-skulled, and the Brachycephalous or short-skulled. Morton names these types respectively the Toltecan and the American proper. The Toltecan type was represented by the primitive inhabitants of Mexico and by the Mound-builders of our Mississippi

Valley; the American proper, by the Indians. The Toltecans made far the closer approach to civilization, though the others possessed a much greater susceptibility therefor than the modern Indians of our prairies would indicate.

Of the Mound-builders painfully little is known. Many of their mounds still remain, not less mysterious or interesting than the pyramids of Egypt, perhaps almost equally ancient. The skeletons exhumed from them often fly into dust as soon as exposed to air, a rare occurrence with the oldest bones found in Europe. On the parapet-crest of the Old Fort at Newark, O., trees certainly five hundred years old have been cut, and they could not have begun their growth till long after the earth-works had been deserted. In some mounds, equally aged trees root in the decayed trunks of a still anterior growth.

Much uncertainty continues to shroud the design of these mounds. Some were for military defence, others for burial places, others for lookout stations, others apparently for religious uses. Still others, it is supposed, formed parts of human dwellings. That they proceeded from intelligence and reflection is clear. Usually, whether they are squares or circles, their construction betrays nice, mathematical exactness, unattainable save by the use of instruments.

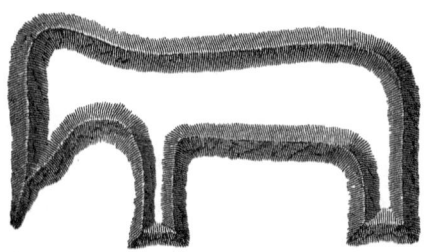

Big Elephant Mound, Wisconsin.

Many constitute effigies—of birds, fishes, quadrupeds, men. In Wisconsin is a mound 135 feet long and well proportioned, much resembling an elephant; in Adams County, O., a gracefully curved serpent, 1,000 feet long, with jaws agape as if to swallow an egg-shaped figure in front; in Granville, in the same State, one in the form of a huge crocodile; in Greenup County, Ky., an image of a bear, which seems leaning forward in an attitude of observation, measuring 53 feet from the top of the back to the end of the foreleg, and 105½ feet from the tip of the nose to the rear of the hind foot.

The sites of towns and cities were artfully selected, near navigable rivers and their confluences, as at Marietta, Cincinnati, and in Kentucky opposite the old mouth of the Scioto. Points for defence were chosen and fortified with scientific precision. The labor expended upon these multitudinous structures must have been enormous, implying a vast population and extensive social, economic, and civil organization. The Cahokia mound, opposite St. Louis, is 90 feet high and 900 feet long.

The Mound-builders made elegant pottery, of various design and accurate shapes, worked bone and all sorts of stones, and even forged copper. There are signs that they understood smelting this metal. They certainly mined it in large quantities, and carried it down the Mississippi hundreds of miles from its source on Lake Superior. They must have been masters of river navigation, but their mode of conveying vast burdens overland, destitute of efficient draft animals as they apparently were, we can hardly even conjecture.

The Mound-builders, as we have said, were related to the antique populations of Mexico and Central America, and the most probable explanation of their departure from their Northern seats is that in face of pestilence, or of some overpowering human foe, they retreated to the Southwest, there to lay, under better auspices, the foundations of new states, and to develop that higher civilization whose relics, too little known, astound the student of the past, as greatly as do the stupendous pillars of Carnac or the grotesque animal figures of Khorsabad and Nimrud.

So much has been written about the American Indians that we need not discuss them at length. They were misnamed Indians by Columbus, who supposed the land he had discovered to be India. At the time of his arrival not more than two hundred thousand of them lived east of the Mississippi, though they were doubtless far more numerous West and South. Whence they came, or whether, if this was a human deed at all, they or another race now extinct drove out the Mound-builders, none can tell.

Of arts the red man had but the rudest. He made wigwams, canoes, bone fish-hooks with lines of hide or twisted bark, stone tomahawks, arrow-heads and spears, clothing of skins, wooden bows, arrows, and clubs. He loved fighting, finery, gambling, and the chase. He domesticated no animals but the dog and possibly the hog. Sometimes brave, he was oftener treacherous, cruel, revengeful. His power of endurance on the trail or the warpath was incredible, and if captured, he let himself be tortured to death without a quiver or a cry. Though superstitious, he believed in a Great Spirit to be worshipped without idols, and in a future life of happy hunting and feasting.

Whether, at the time of which we now

speak, the Indians were an old race, already beginning to decline, or a fresh race, which contact with the whites balked of its development, it is difficult to say. Their career since best accords with the former supposition. In either case we may assume that their national groupings and habitats were nearly the same in 1500 as later, when these became accurately known. In the eighteenth century the Algonquins occupied all the East from Nova Scotia to North Carolina, and stretched west to the Mississippi. At one time they numbered ninety thousand. The Iroquois or Five Nations had their seat in Central and Western New York. North and west of them lived the Hurons or Wyandots. The Appalachians, embracing Cherokees, Creeks, Choctaws, Chickasaws, Seminoles, and a number of lesser tribes, occupied all the southeastern portion of what is now the United States. West of the Mississippi were the Dakotas or Sioux.

Since the white man's arrival upon these shores, very few changes have occurred among the brute inhabitants of North America. A few species, as the Labrador duck and the great auk, have perished. America then possessed but four animals which had appreciable economic value; the dog, the reindeer at the north, which the Mound-builders used as a draft animal but the Indians did not, and the llama and the paco south of the equator. Every one of our present domestic animals originated beyond the Atlantic, being imported hither by our ancestors. The Indians of the lower Mississippi Valley, when De Soto came, had dogs, and also what the Spaniards called hogs, perhaps peccaries, but neither brute was of any breed now bred in the country. A certain kind of dogs were native also to the Juan Fernandez and the Falkland Islands.

Mr. Edward John Payne is doubtless correct in maintaining, in his "History of the New World called America," that the backwardness of the American aborigines was largely due to their lack of animals suitable for draft or travel or producing milk or flesh good for food. From the remotest antiquity Asiatics had the horse, ass, ox and cow, camel and goat—netting ten times the outfit in useful animals which the Peruvians, Mexicans, or Indians enjoyed.

The vegetable kingdom of Old America was equally restricted, which also helps explain its low civilization. At the advent of the Europeans the continent was covered with forests. Then, though a few varieties may have since given out and some imported ones run wild, the undomesticated plants and trees were much as now. Not so the cultivated kinds. The Indians were wretched husbandmen, nor had the Moundbuilders at all the diversity of agricultural products so familiar to us. Tobacco, Indian corn, cocoa, sweet potatoes, potatoes, the custard apple, the Jerusalem artichoke, the guava, the pumpkin and squash, the papaw and the pineapple, indigenous to North America, had been under cultivation here before Columbus came, the first four from most ancient times. The manioc or tapioca-plant, the red-pepper plant, the marmalade plum, and the tomato were raised in South America before 1500. The persimmon, the cinchona tree, millet, the Virginia and the Chili strawberry are natives of this continent, but have been brought under cultivation only within the last three centuries.

The four great cereals, wheat, rye, oats, and rice, constituting all our main food crops but corn, have come to us from Europe. So have cherries, quinces, and pears, also hops, currants, chestnuts, and mushrooms. The banana, regarded by von Humboldt as an original American fruit, modern botanists derive from Asia. With reference to apples there may be some question. Apples of a certain kind flourished in New England so early after the landing of the Pilgrims that it is difficult to suppose the fruit not to have been indigenous to this continent. Champlain, in 1605 or 1606, found the Indians about the present sites of Portland, Boston, and Plymouth in considerable agricultural prosperity, with fields of corn and tobacco, gardens rich in melons, squashes, pumpkins, and beans, the culture of none of which had they apparently learned from white men. Mr. Payne's generalization, that superior food-supply occasioned the Old World's primacy in civilization, and also that of the Mexicans and Peruvians here, seems too sweeping, yet it evidently contains large truth.

PART FIRST

THE FORE-HISTORY

PERIOD I.

DISCOVERY AND SETTLEMENT

1492-1660

CHAPTER I.

COLUMBUS

THERE is no end to the accounts of alleged discoveries of America before Columbus. Most of these are fables. It is, indeed, nearly certain that hardy Basque, Breton, and Norman fishermen, adventuring first far north, then west, had sighted Greenland and Labrador, and become well acquainted with the rich fishing-grounds about Newfoundland and the Saint Lawrence Gulf. Many early charts of these regions, without dates, and hitherto referred to Portuguese navigators of a time so late as 1500, are now thought to be the work of these earlier voyagers. They found the New World, but considered it a part of the Old.

Important, too, is the story of supposed Norse sea-rovers hither, derived from certain Icelandic manuscripts of the fourteenth century. It is a pleasing narrative, that of Lief Ericson's sail in 1000–1001 to Helluland, Markland, and at last to Vineland, and of the subsequent tours by Thorwald Ericson in 1002, Thorfinn Karlsefne, 1007–1009, and of Helge and Finnborge in 1011, to points still farther away. Such voyages probably occurred. As is well known, Helluland has been interpreted to be Newfoundland; Markland, Nova Scotia; and Vineland, the country bordering Mount Hope Bay in Bristol, R. I. These identifications are possibly correct, and even if they are mistaken, Vineland may still have been somewhere upon the coast of what is now the United States.

In the present condition of the evidence, however, we have to doubt this. No scholar longer believes that the writing on Dighton Rock is Norse, or that the celebrated Skeleton in Armor found at Fall River was a Northman's, or that the old Stone Mill at Newport was constructed by men from Iceland. Even if the manuscripts, composed between three and four

Dighton Rock.

hundred years after the events which they are alleged to narrate, are genuine, and if the statements contained in them are true, the latter are far too indefinite to let us be sure that they are applicable to United States localities.

But were we to go so far as to admit that the Northmen came here and began the settlements ascribed to them, they certainly neither appreciated nor published their exploits. Their colony, wherever it was, endured but for a day, and it, with its locality, speedily passed from knowledge in Scandinavia itself. America had not yet, in effect, been discovered.

We must remember that long anterior to Columbus's day unbiassed and thoughtful men had come to believe the earth to be round. They also knew that Europe constituted but a small part of it. In the year 1260 the Venetian brothers Niccolo and Maffeo Polo made their way to China, the first men from Western Europe ever to travel so far. They returned in 1269, but in 1271 set out again, accompanied by Niccolo's son, a youth of seventeen. This son was the famous Marco Polo, whose work,

The Old Stone Mill at Newport, R. I.

"The Wonders of the World," reciting his extended journeys through China and the extreme east and southeast of Asia, and his eventful voyage home by sea, ending in 1295, has come down to our time, one of the most interesting volumes in the world. Friar Orderic's eastern travels in 1322–1330, as appropriated by Sir John Mandeville, were published before 1371.

Columbus knew these writings, and the reading and re-reading of them had made him an enthusiast. In Polo's book he had learned of Mangi and Far Cathay, with their thousands of gorgeous cities, the meanest finer than any then in Europe; of their abounding mines pouring forth infinite wealth, their noble rivers, happy populations, curious arts, and benign government. Polo had told him of Cambalu (Peking), winter residence of the Great Khan, Kublai—Cambalu with its palaces of marble, golden-roofed, its guard of ten thousand soldiers, its imperial stables containing five thousand elephants, its unnumbered army, navy, and merchant marine; of oxen huge as elephants; of richest spices, nuts large as melons, canes fifteen yards long,

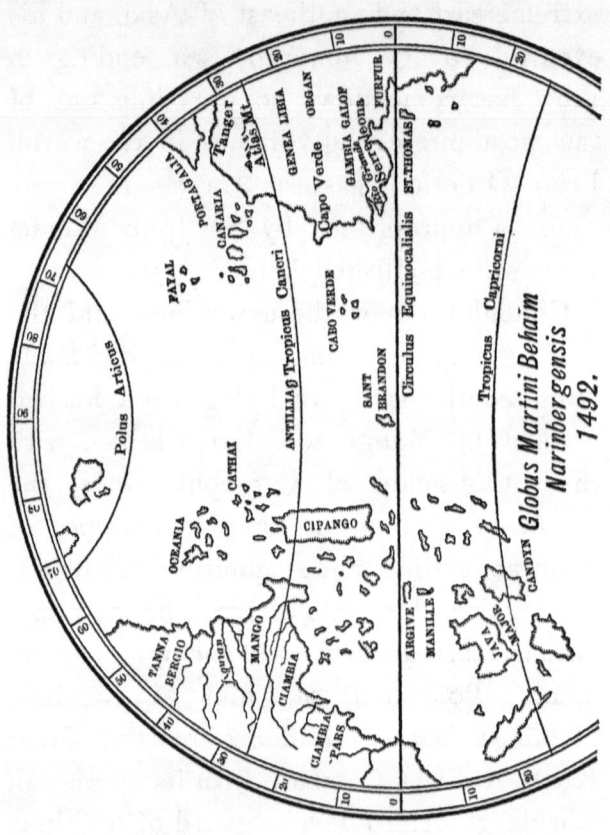

silks, cambrics, and the choicest furs; and of magic Cipango (Japan), island of pearls, whose streets were paved with gold.

Columbus believed all this, and it co-operated with his intense and even bigoted religious faith to kindle in him an all-consuming ambition to reach this distant Eden by sea, that he might carry the Gospel to those opulent heathen and partake their unbounded temporal riches in return. Poor specimen of a saint as Columbus is now known to have been, he believed himself divinely called to this grand enterprise.

Christopher Columbus, or Christobal Colon, as he always signed himself after he entered the service of Spain, was born in Genoa about 1456. Little is certainly known of his early life. His father was a humble wool-carder. The youth possessed but a sorry education, spite of his few months at the University of Pavia. At the age of fourteen he became a sailor, knocking about the world in the roughest manner, half the time practically a pirate. In an all-day's sea fight, once, his ship took fire and he had to leap overboard; but being a strong swimmer he swam, aided by an oar, eight leagues to land.

From 1470 to 1484 we find him in Portugal, the country most interested and engaged then in ocean-going and discovery. Here he must have known Martin Behem, author of the famous globe, finished in 1492, whereon Asia is exhibited as reaching far into the same hemisphere with Europe. Prince Henry of Portugal earnestly patronized all schemes for exploration and discovery, and the daughter, Philippa, of one of his captains, Perestrello, Columbus married. With her he lived at Porto Santo in the Madeiras, where he became familiar with Correo, her sister's husband, also a distinguished navigator. The islanders fully believed in the existence of lands in the western Atlantic. West winds had brought to them strange woods curiously carved, huge cane-brakes like those of India described by Ptolemy, peculiarly fashioned canoes, and corpses with skin of a hue unknown to Europe or Africa.

Reflecting on these things, studying Perestrello's and Correo's charts and accounts of their voyages, corresponding with

Prince Henry of Portugal—"The Navigator."

From an old print.

Toscanelli and other savans, himself an adept in drawing maps and sea-charts, for a time his occupation in Lisbon, cruising here and there, once far northward to Iceland, and talking with navigators from every Atlantic port, Columbus became acquainted with the best geographical science of his time.

This had convinced him that India could be reached by sailing westward. The theoretical possibility of so doing was of course admitted by all who held the earth to be a sphere, but most regarded it practically impossible, in the then condition of navigation, to sail the necessary distance. Columbus considered the earth far smaller than was usually thought, a belief which we find hinted at so early as 1447, upon the famous *mappe-monde* of the Pitti Palace in Florence, whereon Europe appears projected far round to the northwest. Columbus seems to have viewed this extension as a sort of yoke joining India to Scandinavia by the north. He judged that Asia, or at least Cipango, stretched two-thirds of the way to

Europe, India being twice as near westward as eastward. Thirty or forty days he deemed sufficient for making it. Toscanelli and Behem as well as he held this belief; he dared boldly to act upon it.

Queen Isabella of Spain.

But to do so required resources. There are indications that Columbus at some time, perhaps more than once, urged his scheme upon Genoa and Venice. If so it was in vain. Nor can we tell whether such an attempt, if made, was earlier or later than his plea before the court of Portugal, for this cannot be dated. The latter was probably in 1484. King John II. was impressed, and referred Columbus's scheme to a council of his wisest advisers, who denounced it as visionary. Hence in 1485 or 1486 Columbus proceeded to Spain to lay his project before Ferdinand and Isabella.

On the way he stopped at a Franciscan convent near Palos, begging bread for himself and son. The Superior, Marchena, became interested in him, and so did one of the Pinzons—famous navigators of Palos. The king and queen were at the time holding court at Cordova, and thither Columbus went, fortified with a recommendation from Marchena. The monarchs were engrossed in the final conquest of Granada, and Columbus had to wait through six weary and heart-sickening years before royal attention was turned to his cause. It must have been during this delay that he despatched his brother Bartholomew to England with an appeal to Henry VII. Christopher had brought Alexander Geraldinus, the scholar, and also the Archbishop of Toledo, to espouse his mission, and finally, at the latter's instance, Ferdinand, as John of Portugal

Columbus begging at the Franciscan Convent.

had done, went so far as to convene, at Salamanca, a council of reputed scholars to pass judgment upon Columbus and his proposition. By these, as by the Portuguese, he was declared a misguided enthusiast. They were too much behind the age even to admit the spherical figure of the earth. According to Scripture, they said, the earth is flat, adding that it was contrary to reason for men to walk heads downward, or snow and rain to ascend, or trees to grow with their roots upward.

The war for Granada ended, Santangel and others of his converts at court secured Columbus an interview with Isabella, but his demands seeming to her arrogant, he was dismissed. Nothing daunted, the hero had started for France, there to plead as he had pleaded in Portugal and Spain already, when to his joy a messenger overtook him with orders to come once more before the queen.

Fuller thought and argument had convinced this eminent woman that the experiment urged by Columbus ought to be tried, and a contract was soon concluded, by which, on condition that he should bear one-eighth the expense of the expedition, the public chest of Castile was to furnish the remainder. The story of the crown jewels having been pledged for this purpose is now discredited. If such pledging occurred, it was earlier, in prosecuting the war with the Moors. The whole sum needed for the voyage was about fifty thousand dollars. Columbus was made admiral, also viceroy of whatever lands should be discovered, and he was to have ten per cent. of all the revenues from such lands. For his contribution to the outfit he was indebted to the Pinzons.

This arrangement was made in April or May, 1492, and on the third of the next August, after the utmost difficulty in shipping crews for this sail into the sea of darkness, Columbus put out from Palos with one hundred and twenty men, on three ships. These were the Santa Maria, the Niña, and the Pinta. The largest, the Santa Maria, was of not over one hundred tons, having a deck-length of sixty-three feet, a keel of fifty-one feet, a draft of

Embarkation of Christopher Columbus at Palos.

From an old print.

ten feet six inches, and her mast-head sixty feet above sea-level. She probably had four anchors, with hemp cables.

From Palos they first bore southward to the Canary Islands, into the track of the prevalent east winds, then headed west, for Cipango, as Columbus supposed, but really toward the northern part of Florida. When a little beyond what he regarded the longitude of Cipango, noticing the flight of birds to the southwest, he was induced to follow these, which accident made his landfall occur at Guanahani (San Salvador), in the Bahamas, instead of the Florida coast

Near midnight, between October 11th and 12th, Columbus, being on the watch, descried a light ahead. About two o'clock on the morning of the 12th the lookout on the Pinta distinctly saw land through the moonlight. When it was day they went on shore. The 12th of October, 1492, therefore, was the date on which for the first time, so far as history attests with assurance, a European foot pressed the soil of this continent. Adding nine days to this to translate it into New Style, we have October 21st as the day answering to that on which Columbus first became sure that his long toil and watching had not been in vain.

The admiral having failed to note its latitude and longitude, it is not known which of the Bahamas was the San Salvador of Columbus, whether Grand Turk Island, Cat (the present San Salvador), Watling, Mariguana, Acklin, or Samana, though the last named well corresponds with his description. Mr. Justin Winsor, however, and with him a majority of the latest critics, believes that Watling's Island was the place. Before returning to Spain, Columbus discovered Cuba, and also Hayti or Espagñola (Hispaniola), on the latter of which islands he built a fort.

In a second voyage, from Cadiz, 1493–1496, the great explorer discovered the Lesser Antilles and Jamaica. In a third, 1498–1500, he came upon Trinidad and the mainland of South America, at the mouth of the Orinoco. This was later by thirteen months and a week than the Cabots' landfall at Labrador or Nova Scotia, though a year before Amerigo Vespucci saw the coast of Brazil. It was during this third absence that Columbus, hated as an Italian and for his undeniable greed, was superseded by Bobadilla, who sent him and his brother home in chains. Soon free again, he sets off in 1502 upon a fourth cruise, in which he reaches the coast of Honduras.

To the day of his death, however, the discoverer of America never suspected that he had brought to light a new continent. Even during this his last expedition he maintained that the coast he had touched was that of Mangi, contiguous to Cathay, and that nineteen days of travel overland would have taken him to the Ganges. He arrived in Spain on September 12, 1504, and died at Segovia on May 20th of the next year. His bones are believed to rest in the cathedral at Santo Domingo, transported thither in 1541, the Columbus-remains till recently at Havana being those of his son Diego. The latter, under the belief that they were the father's, were transferred to Genoa in 1887, and deposited there on July 2d of that year with the utmost ecclesiastical pomp.

As Columbus was ignorant of having found a new continent, so was he denied the honor of giving it a name, this falling by accident, design, or carelessness of truth, to Amerigo Vespucci, a native of Florence, whose active years were spent in Spain and Portugal. Vespucci made three voyages into the western seas. In the second, 1501, he visited the coast of Brazil, and pushed farther south than any navigator had yet done, probably so far as the island of South Georgia, in latitude 54°. His account of this voyage found its way into print in 1504, at Augsburg, Germany, the first published narrative of any discovery of the mainland. Although, as above noted, it was not the earliest discovery of the main, it was widely regarded such, and caused Vespucci to be named for many years as the peer, if not the superior of Columbus. The publication ran through many editions.

Amerigo Vespucci.

Fac-simile of an old print.

That of Strassburg, 1505, mentioned Vespucci on its title-page as having discovered a new "Southern Land." This is the earliest known utterance hinting at the continental nature of the new discovery, as separate from Asia, an idea which grew into a conviction only after Magellan's voyage, described in the next chapter. In 1507 appeared at St. Dié, near Strassburg, a four-page pamphlet by one Lud, secretary to the Duke of Lorraine, describing Vespucci's voyages and speaking of the Indians as the "American race." This pamphlet came out the same year in another form, as part of a book entitled "Introduction to Cosmography," prepared by Martin Waldseemüller, under the *nom de plume* of "Hylacomylus." In this book the new "part of the world" is distinctly called "THE LAND OF AMERICUS, OR AMERICA." There is some evidence that Vespucci at least connived at the misapprehension which brought him his renown—as undeserved as it has become permanent—but this cannot be regarded as proved.

CHAPTER II.

EARLY SPANISH AMERICA

As we have seen, Spain by no means deserves the entire credit of bringing the western continent to men's knowledge. Columbus himself was an Italian. So was Marco Polo, his inspirer, and also Toscanelli, his instructor, by whose chart he sailed his ever-memorable voyage. To Portugal as well Columbus was much indebted, despite his rebuff there. Portugal then led the world in the art of navigation and in enthusiasm for discovery. Nor, probably, would Columbus have asked her aid in vain, had she not previously committed herself to the enterprise of reaching India eastward, a purpose brilliantly fulfilled when, in 1498, Vasco da Gama rounded the Cape of Good Hope and sailed to Calicut, on the coast of Malabar. Already before

Vasco da Gama.

From an old print.

this Spain and Portugal were rivals in the search for new lands, and Pope Alexander VI. had had to be appealed to, to fix their fields. By his bull of May 3, 4, 1493, he ordained as the separating line the meridian passing through a point one hundred leagues west of the Azores, where Columbus had observed the needle of his compass to point without deflection toward the north star. Portugal objecting to this boundary as excluding her from the longitude of the newly found Indies, by the treaty of Tordesillas, June 7, 1494, the two powers, with the Pope's assent, moved the line two hundred and seventy leagues still farther west. At this time neither party dreamed of the complications destined subsequently to arise in reference to the position of this meridian on the other side of the globe.

The meridian of the Tordesillas convention had been supposed still to give Spain all the American discoveries likely to be made, it being ascertained only later that by it Portugal had obtained a considerable part of the South American mainland.

Brazil, we know, was, till in 1822 it became independent, a Portuguese dependency. Spain, however, retained both groups of the Antilles with the entire main about the Gulf of Mexico, and became the earliest great principality in the western world.

Before the death of Columbus, Spain had taken firm possession of Cuba, Porto Rico, and St. Domingo, and she stood ready to seize any of the adjoining islands or lands so soon as gold, pearls, or aught else of value should be found there. Cruises of discovery were made in every direction, first, indeed, in Central and South America.

In 1506 de Solis sailed along the eastern coast of Yucatan. In 1513 the governor of a colony on the Isthmus of Darien, Vasco Nuñez de Balboa, from the top of a lofty mountain on the isthmus, saw what is now called the Pacific Ocean. He designated it the South Sea, a name which it habitually bore till far into the eighteenth century. From this time the exploration and settlement of the western coast, both up and down, went on with little interruption, but

Balboa discovering the Pacific Ocean.

this history, somewhat foreign to our theme, we cannot detail.

The same year, 1513, Ponce de Leon, an old Spanish soldier in the wars with the Moors, a companion of Columbus in his second voyage, and till now governor of

Ponce de Leon.

Porto Rico, began exploration to the northward. Leaving Porto Rico with three ships, he landed on the coast of an unknown country, where he thought to find not only infinite gold but also the much-talked-about fountain of perpetual youth.

His landing occurred on Easter Sunday, or *Pascua Florida*, March 27, 1513, and so he named the country Florida. The place was a few miles north of the present town of St. Augustine. Exploring the coast around the southern extremity of the peninsula, he sailed among a group of islands, which he designated the Tortugas. Returning to Porto Rico, he was appointed governor of the new country. He made a second voyage, was attacked by the natives and mortally wounded, and returned to Cuba to die.

Juan de Grijalva explored the south coast of the Gulf of Mexico, from Yucatan toward the Panuco. Interest attaches to this enterprise mainly because the treasure which Grijalva collected aroused the envy and greed of the future conqueror of Mexico, Hernando Cortez.

In 1518, Velasquez, governor of Cuba, sends Cortez westward, with eleven ships and over six hundred men, for the purpose of exploration. He landed at Tabasco, thence proceeded to the Island of San Juan de Ulúa, nearly opposite Vera Cruz, where

Hernando Cortes.
From an old print.

he received messengers and gifts from the Emperor Montezuma. Ordered to leave the country, he destroyed his ships and marched directly upon the capital. He seized Montezuma and held him as a hostage for the peaceable conduct of his subjects. The Mexicans took up arms, only to be defeated again and again by the Spaniards. Montezuma became a vassal of the Spanish crown, and covenanted to pay annual tribute. Attempting to reconcile his people to this agreement he was himself assailed and wounded, and, refusing all nourishment, soon after died. With reenforcements, Cortez completed the conquest of the country, and Mexico became a province of Spain.

Vasquez de Ayllon, one of the auditors of the Island of Santo Domingo, sent two ships from that island to the Bahamas for Indians to be sold as slaves. Driven from their course by the wind, they at length reached the shore of South Carolina, at the mouth of the Wateree River, which they named the Jordan, calling the country

Chicora. Though kindly treated by the natives, the ruthless adventurers carried away some seventy of these. One ship was lost, and most of the captives on the others died during the voyage. Vasquez was, by the Emperor Charles V., King of Spain, made governor of this new province, and again set sail to take possession. But the natives, in revenge for the cruel treatment which they had previously received, made a furious attack upon the invaders. The few survivors of the slaughter returned to Santo Domingo, and the expedition was abandoned. These voyages were in 1520 and 1526.

In connection with the subject of Spanish voyages, a passing notice should be given to one, who, though not of Spanish birth, yet did much to further the progress of discovery on the part of his adopted country. Magellan was a Portuguese navigator who had been a child when Columbus came back in triumph from the West Indies. Refused consideration from King Emmanuel, of Portugal, for a wound re-

Montezuma mortally wounded by his own subjects.

ceived under his flag during the war against Morocco, he renounced his native land and offered his services to the sagacious Charles V., of Spain, who gladly accepted them. With a magnificent fleet, Magellan, in 1519, set sail from Seville, cherishing Columbus's bold purpose, which no one had yet realized, of reaching the East Indies by a westward voyage. After touching at the Canaries, he explored the coast of South America, passed through the strait now called by his name, discovered the Ladrone Islands, and christened the circumjacent ocean the Pacific.

The illustrious navigator now sailed for the Philippine Islands, so named from Philip, son of Charles V., who succeeded that monarch as Philip II. By the Tordesillas division above described, the islands were properly in the Portuguese hemisphere, but on the earliest maps, made by Spaniards, they were placed twenty-five degrees too far east, and this circumstance, whether accidental or designed, has preserved them to Spain even to the present time. At the Philippine Islands Magellan was killed in an affray with the natives. One of his ships, the Victoria, after sailing around the Cape of Good Hope, arrived in Spain, having been the first to circumnavigate the globe. The voyage had taken three years and twenty-eight days.

The disastrous failure of the expedition of Vasquez de Ayllon to Florida did not discourage attempts on the part of others in the same direction. Velaspuez, governor of Cuba, jealous of the success of Cortez in Mexico, had sent Pamphilo de Narvaez to arrest him. In this attempt Narvaez had been defeated and taken prisoner. Undeterred by this failure he had solicited and received of Charles V. the position of governor over Florida, a territory at that time embracing the whole southern part of what is now the United States, and reaching from Cape Sable to the Panuco, or River of Palms, in Mexico. With three hundred men he, in 1528, landed near Appalachee Bay, and marched inland with the hope of opening a country rich and populous.

Death of Magellan.

Bitterly was he disappointed. Swamps and forests, wretched wigwams with their squalid inmates everywhere met his view, but no gold was to be found. Discouraged, he and his followers returned to the coast, where almost superhuman toil and

Ferdinand de Soto.

skill enabled them to build five boats, in which they hoped to work westward to the Spanish settlements. Embarking, they stole cautiously along the coast for some distance, but were at last driven by a storm upon an island, perhaps Galveston, perhaps Santa Rosa, where Narvaez and most of his men perished. Four of his followers survived to cross Texas to the Gulf of California and reach the town of San Miguel on the west coast of Mexico. Here they found their countrymen, searching as usual for pearls, gold, and slaves, and by their help they made a speedy return to Spain, heroes of as remarkable an adventure as history records. These unfortunates were the first Europeans to visit New Mexico. Their narrative led to the exploration of that country by Coronado and others, and to the discoveries of Cortez in Lower California.

Ferdinand de Soto, eager to rival the exploits of Cortez in Mexico, and of his former commander, Pizarro, in Peru, offered to conquer Florida at his own expense. Appointed governor-general of Florida and of Cuba, he sailed with seven large and three small vessels. From Espiritu Santo Bay he, in 1539, marched with six hundred men into the country of the Appalachians and discovered the harbor of Pensacola. After wintering at Appalachee he set out into the interior, said to abound in gold and silver. Penetrating northeasterly as far as the Savannah, he found only copper and mica. From here he marched first northwest into northern central Georgia, then southwest into Alabama. A battle was fought with the natives at Mavila, or

A Palisaded Indian Town in Alabama.

Mobile, in which the Spaniards suffered serious loss. Ships that he had ordered arrived at Pensacola, but de Soto determined not to embark until success should have crowned his efforts. He turned back into the interior, into the country of the Chickasaws, marched diagonally over the present State of Mississippi to its northwest corner, and crossed the Mississippi River near the lowest Chickasaw Bluff. From this point the general direction of the Spanish progress was southwest, through what is now Arkansas, past the site of Little Rock, till at last a river which seems to have been the Washita was reached. Down this stream de Soto and his decimated force floated—two hundred and fifty of his men had succumbed to the hardships and perils of his march—arriving at the junction of the Red with the Mississippi River on Sunday, April 17, 1542. At this point de Soto sickened and died, turning over the command to Luis de Moscoso. Burying their late leader's corpse at night deep in the bosom of the great river, and constructing themselves boats, the survivors of this ill-fated expedition, now reduced to three hundred and seventy-two persons, made the best of their way down the Mississippi to the Gulf, and along its coast, finally reaching the Spanish town near the mouth of the Panuco in Mexico.

Thus no settlement had as yet been made in Florida by the Spanish. The first occupation destined to be permanent was brought about through religious jealousy inspired by the establishment of a French Protestant (Huguenot) colony in the terri-

Burial of de Soto in the Mississippi at night.

tory. Ribault, a French captain commissioned by Charles IX., was put in command of an expedition by that famous Huguenot, Admiral Coligny, and landed on the coast of Florida, at the mouth of the St. John's, which he called the River of May. This was in 1562. The name Carolina, which that section still bears, was given to a fort at Port Royal, or St. Helena. Ribault returned to France, where civil war was then raging between the Catholics and the Protestants or Huguenots. His colony, waiting

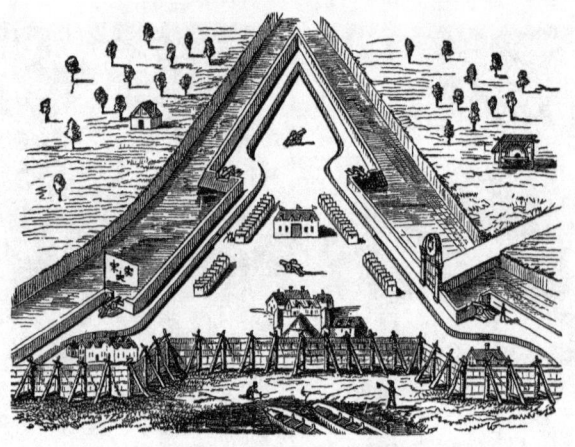

Fort Carolina on the River of May.

for promised aid and foolishly making no attempt to cultivate the soil, soon languished. Dissensions arose, and an effort was made to return home. Famine having carried off the greater number, the colony came to an end. In 1564 Coligny sent out Laudonnière, who built another fort, also named Carolina, on the River of May. Again misfortunes gathered thickly about the settlers, when Ribault arrived bringing supplies.

But Spain claimed this territory, and Pedro Melendez a Spanish soldier, was in

Pedro Melendez.

1565 sent by Philip II. to conquer it from the French, doubly detested as Protestants. He landed in the harbor and at the mouth of the river, to both of which he gave the name St. Augustine. Melendez lost no time in attacking Fort Carolina, which he surprised, putting the garrison mercilessly to the sword. The destruction of the French colony was soon after avenged by Dominic de Gourgues, who sailed from France to punish the enemies of his country. Having accomplished his purpose by the slaughter of the Spanish garrison he returned home, but the French Protestants made no further effort to colonize Florida.

Spain claimed the land by right of discovery, but, although maintaining the feeble settlement at St. Augustine, did next to nothing after this to explore or civilize this portion of America. The nation that had sent out Columbus was not destined to be permanently the great power of the New World. The hap of first landing upon the Antilles, and also the warm climate and the peaceable nature of the aborigines, led Spain to fix her settlements in latitudes that were too low for the best health and the greatest energy. Most of the settlers were of a wretched class, criminals and adventurers, and they soon mixed largely with the natives. Spain herself greatly lacked in vigor, partly from national causes,

Indians devoured by dogs.

From an old print.

partly from those obscure general causes which even to this day keep Latin Europe, in military power and political accomplishments, inferior to Teutonic or Germanic Europe.

Moreover, the Spaniards found their first American conquests too easy, and the rewards of these too great. This prevented all thought of developing the country through industry, concentrating expectation solely upon waiting fortunes, to be had from the natives by the sword or through forced labor in mines. Their treatment of the aborigines was nothing short of diabolical. Well has it been said: "The Spaniards had sown desolation, havoc, and misery in and around their track. They had depopulated some of the best peopled of the islands and renewed them with victims deported from others. They had inflicted upon hundreds of thousands of the natives all the forms and agonies of fiendish cruelty, driving them to self-starvation and suicide, as a way of mercy and release from an utterly wretched existence. They had come to be viewed by their victims as fiends of hate, malignity, and all dark and cruel desperation and mercilessness in passion. The hell which they denounced upon their victims was shorn of its worst terror by the assurance that these tormentors were not to be there. Las Casas, the noble missionary, the true soldier of the cross, and the few priests and monks who sympathized with him, in vain protested against these cruelties."

To all these causes we must add the narrow colonial policy of Spain. Imitating Venice and ancient Carthage instead of Greece, she held her dependencies under the straitest servitude to herself as conquered provinces, repressing all political or commercial independence. A similar restrictive policy, indeed, hampered the colonies of other nations, but it was nowhere else so irrational or blighting as in Spanish America.

CHAPTER III.

EXPLORATION AND COLONIZATION BY THE FRENCH AND THE ENGLISH

How the French fought for foothold in Florida and were routed by the Spaniards has just been related. So early as 1504, and possibly much earlier, before Cabot or Columbus, French sailors were familiar with the fisheries of Newfoundland. To the Isle of Cape Breton they gave its name in remembrance of their own Brittany. The attention of the French Government was thus early directed toward America, and it at length determined to share in the new discoveries along with the Spanish and the English.

In 1524 Verrazano, a Florentine navigator, was sent by Francis I. on a voyage of discovery to the New World. Sighting the shores of America near the present

Wilmington, North Carolina, he explored the coast of New Jersey, touched land near New York Bay, and anchored a few days in the harbor of Newport. In this vicinity he came upon an island, which was

Verrazano, the Florentine Navigator.

probably Block Island. Sailing from here along the coast as far north as Newfoundland, he named this vast territory New France.

In 1534 Cartier, a noted voyager of St. Malo, coasted along the north of New-

Jacques Cartier.
From an old print.

foundland, passed through the Straits of Belle Isle into the water now known as St. Lawrence Gulf, and into the mouth of the St. Lawrence River. Erecting a cross, he took possession of the shores in the name of the king of France.

In the following year he made a second voyage, going up as far as the mouth of a small river which the year before he had named St. John's. He called the waters the Bay of St. Lawrence. Ascending this, he came to a settlement of the natives near a certain hill, which he called *Mont Royal*, now modified into "Montreal." Cartier returned to France in 1536, only a few of his men having survived the winter.

In 1540 Lord Roberval fitted out a fleet, with Cartier as subordinate. Cartier sailed at once—his third voyage—Roberval following the next year. A fort was built near the present site of Quebec. Roberval and Cartier disagreed and returned to France, leaving the real foundation of Quebec to be laid by Champlain, much later.

In 1604 De Monts arrived on the coast of Nova Scotia and erected a fort at the mouth of the St. Croix, New Brunswick. He also made a settlement on the shore of the present harbor of Annapolis, naming it Port Royal, and the country around it Acadia. De Monts is famous largely because under him the Sieur de Champlain, the real father of French colonization in America, began his illustrious career. He had entered the St. Lawrence in 1603. In 1608 he founded Quebec, the first permanent colony of New France. The next year he explored the lake which perpetuates his name. In 1615 he saw Lake Huron, Le Caron, the Franciscan, preceding him in this only by a few days. Fired with ardor for discovery, Champlain joined the Hurons in an attack upon the Iroquois. This led him into what is now New York State, but whether the Indian camp first attacked by him was on Onondaga or on Canandaigua Lake is still in debate. These were but the beginning of Champlain's travels, by which many other

Frenchmen, some as missionaries, some as traders, were inspired to press far out into the then unknown West. We shall resume the narrative in Chapter VII. of the next period. Champlain died at Quebec in 1635.

Turn back now to Columbus's time. England, destined to dominate the continent of North America, was also practically the discoverer of the same. On St. John's day, June 24, 1497, thirteen months and a week before Columbus saw South America, John Cabot, a Venetian in the service of King Henry VII., from the deck of the good ship Matthew, of Bristol, descried land somewhere on the coast either of Labrador or of Nova Scotia. Cabot, of course, supposed this *prima vista* of his to belong to Asia, and expected to reach Cipango next voyage. So late as 1543 Jean Allefonsce, on reaching New England, took it for the border of Tartary. André Thevet, in 1515, in a pretended voyage to Maine, places Cape Breton on the west coast of Asia. This confusion probably explains the tradition of Norumbega as a great city, and of other populous and wealthy cities in the newly found land. Men transferred ideas of Eastern Asia to this American shore.

The subsequent year Cabot made a second voyage, inspecting the American coast northward till icebergs were met, southward to the vicinity of Albemarle Sound. Possibly in his first expedition, probably in the second, John Cabot was accompanied by his more famous son, Sebastian. For many years after the Cabots, England made little effort to explore the New World. Henry VII. was a Catholic. He therefore submitted to the Pope's bull which gave America to Spain. Henry VIII. had married Catherine of Aragon. He allowed Ferdinand, her father, to employ the skill and daring of Sebastian Cabot in behalf of Spain. It was reserved for the splendid reign of Elizabeth to show what English courage and endurance could accomplish in extending England's power.

Sebastian Cabot.

From an old print.

Like those before him, Martin Frobisher was in earnest to find the northwest passage, in whose existence all navigators then fully believed. Like Columbus, he vainly sought friends to aid him. At last, after he had waited fifteen years in vain, Dudley, the Earl of Warwick, helped him to an outfit. His little fleet embraced the Gabriel, of thirty-five tons, the Michael of thirty, and a pinnace of ten. As it swept to sea past Greenwich, the Queen waved her hand in token of good-will. Sailing northward near the Shetland Isles, Frobisher passed the southern shore of Greenland and came in sight of Labrador, 1576.

He effected a landing at Hall's Island, at the mouth of the bay now called by his name, but which he thought to be a strait, his discovery thus strengthening his belief in the possibility of reaching Asia by this westward course. He sailed up the bay as far as Butcher's Island, where five of his men were taken prisoners by the natives. All effort to rescue them was made, but to no purpose. Among the curiosities which he brought home was a piece of stone, or black ore, which gave rise to the belief that gold was to be found in this new country.

A second and larger expedition sailed in 1577. The Queen gave £1,000 and lent the royal ship Aid, of two hundred tons. The Gabriel and the Michael of the former year were again made ready, besides smaller craft. This voyage was to seek gold rather than to discover the northwest passage. The fleet set sail May 27th, and on July 18th arrived off North Foreland, or Hall's Island, so named for the man who had brought away the piece of black earth. Search was made for this metal, supposed to be so valuable, and large quantities were found. The fleet sailed back to England with a heavy cargo of it.

In 1578 a third and the last voyage was made to this region, to which the name *meta incognita* was given. Two large ships were furnished by the Queen, and these were accompanied by thirteen smaller ones.

It was now the purpose to found a colony. The expedition set sail May 31st, going through the English Channel, and reaching the coast of Greenland June 21st. Frobisher and a few of his sailors landed where, perhaps, white men had never trodden before. As he came near the bay he was driven south by stormy weather, and entered, not knowing his whereabouts, the waters of Hudson's Straits, which he traversed a distance of sixty miles. He succeeded at length in retracing his course, and anchored on the southern shore of Frobisher's Bay, in the Countess of Warwick's Sound. But the desire for gold, the bleak winds, barren shores, and drifting icebergs, all combined to dispel the hopes of making a successful settlement, and the adventurers turned their faces homeward, carrying once more a cargo of ore, which proved, like the first, to be of no value whatever.

Almost three hundred years later Captain Hall, the American explorer, visited the Countess's Island and Sound. Among the Eskimos, from 1860 to 1862, he learned

106 DISCOVERY AND SETTLEMENT [1578

An Indian Village at the Roanoke Settlement.

the tradition of Frobisher's visits, which
had been preserved and handed down.
They knew the number of ships; they
spoke of the three times that white men

had come; how five of these strangers had been taken captive, and how, after remaining through the winter, they had been allowed to build a boat, and to launch themselves upon the icy seas, never to be heard of more. Captain Hall was shown many relics of Frobisher's voyages, some of which he sent to the Royal Geographical Society of London, a part to the Smithsonian Institute at Washington. The small English house of lime and stone on this island was still standing in good condition, and there was also a trench where they had built their ill-fated boat.

A contemporary of Frobisher, Sir Francis Drake, also entertained the idea of making the northwest passage. While engaged in privateering or piratical expeditions against the Spanish, Drake landed on the Isthmus of Panama, saw the Pacific for the first time, and determined to enter it by the Straits of Magellan. In 1577 he made his way through the straits, plundered the Spanish along the coast of Chili and Peru, and sailed as far north as the 48th parallel, or Oregon, calling the country New Albion. Steering homeward by the Cape of Good Hope, he arrived at Plymouth, his starting-point, in 1580, having been absent about two years and ten months.

Sir Humphrey Gilbert.

Thomas Cavendish had been with Grenville in the voyage of 1585 to Virginia. Frobisher's attempts inspired him with the ambition of the age. In 1586 he, too, sailed through the Straits of Magellan, burning and plundering Spanish ships, rounded the

Sir Walter Raleigh.

From a portrait attributed to Zuccaro in the National Portrait Gallery, London.

Cape of Good Hope, and reached Plymouth in 1588, having been gone about two years and fifty days.

These half-piratical attempts against Spain led continually into American waters, till the notion of forming a permanent outpost here as base for such adventures suggested to Sir Humphrey Gilbert the plan, which he failed to realize, of founding an American settlement. Gilbert visited our shores in 1579, and again in 1583, but was lost on his return from the latter voyage.

In 1584 Sir Walter Raleigh sent two captains, Amidas and Barlow, to inspect the coast off what is now North Carolina. They reported so favorably that he began, next year, a colony on Roanoke Island. England was now a Protestant land, and no longer heeded Spanish claims to the transatlantic continent, save so far as actual settlements had been made.

Sir Richard Grenville commanded this expedition, but was to return on seeing the one hundred and eight colonists who accompanied him well established. Queen

Elizabeth gave the name VIRGINIA to the new country. Drake, tending homeward from one of his raids on the Spanish coast,

Queen Elizabeth.

in 1586, offered the settlers supplies, but finding them wholly discouraged, he carried them back to England.

Determined to plant an agricultural community, Raleigh next time, 1587, sent men with their families. A daughter to one of these, named Dare, was the first child of English parents born in America. Becoming destitute, the colony despatched its governor home for supplies. He returned to find the settlement deserted, and no tidings as to the fate of the poor colonists have ever been heard from that day to our own. The Jamestown settlers mentioned in the next chapter found among their Indian neighbors a boy whose whitish complexion and wavy hair induced the interesting suspicion that he was descended from some one of these lost colonists of Roanoke.

Thus Sir Walter's enterprise had to be abandoned. In the £40,000 spent upon it his means were exhausted. Besides, England was now at war with Spain, and the entire energies of the nation were in requisition for the overthrow of the Spanish Armada.

CHAPTER IV.

THE PLANTING OF VIRGINIA

WE have now arrived at the seventeenth century. In 1606 King James I. issued the first English colonial charter. It created a first and a second Virginia Company, the one having its centre in London, and coming to be known as the London Company; the other made up of Bristol, Exeter, and Plymouth men, and gradually taking the title of the Plymouth Company. This latter company, the second, or Plymouth Company, authorized to plant between 38° and 45° north, effected a settlement in 1607 at the mouth of the Kennebec River. Little came of it but suffering, the colonists, after a severe winter, returning to England.

A colony of one hundred and five planters sent out by the first or London Company, proceeded, also in 1607, to Chesa-

King James I.

Mr. Henry Irving's Collection.

peake Bay, entering James River, to which they indeed gave this name, and planted upon its banks Jamestown, the first permanent English colony on the continent. This London Company consisted of a council in England, appointed by the king, having the power to name the members of a local council which was to govern the colony, the colonists themselves having no voice.

It is well known that the very earliest population of the Old Dominion was not of the highest, but predominantly idle and thriftless. Vagabonds and homeless children picked up in the streets of London, as well as some convicts, were sent to the colony from England to be indented as servants, permanently, or for a term of years. Persons of the better class, to be sure, came as well, and the quality of the population, on the whole, improved year by year. Settlement here followed a centrifugal tendency, except as this was repressed by fear of the Indians. In 1616 the departments of Virginia were Henrico, up the James above the Appomattox mouth, West and Shirley Hundreds, Jamestown, Kiquoton, and King's Gift on the coast near Cape Charles—a wide reach of territory to be covered by a total population of only three hundred and fifty.

A little exporting was immediately begun. So early as May 20, 1608, Jamestown sent to England a ship laden with iron ore, sassafras, cedar posts, and walnut boards. Another followed on June 2d, with a cargo all of cedar wood. This year or the next, small quantities of pitch, tar, and glass were sent. From 1619 tobacco was so common as to be the currency. About 1650 it was largely exported, a million and a half pounds, on the average, yearly. The figure had risen to twelve million pounds by 1670. At the middle of the century, corn, wheat, rice, hemp, flax, and fifteen varieties of fruit, as well as excellent wine were produced. A wind-mill was set up about 1620, the first in America. It stood at Falling Creek on the James River. The pioneer iron works on the continent were in this colony, hailing from about the date last named. Community of property prevailed at Jamestown in all the earliest years, as it did at Plymouth. After the **event** noted by John Rolfe: "about the last of August [1619] came in a Dutch man of warre that sold us twenty Negars," slavery was a continual and increasing curse, as is attested by the laws concerning slaves. It encouraged indolence and savagery of habit and nature. Virginian slaves, however, were better treated than those farther south. They were tolerably clothed, fed, and housed.

Tobacco Plant.

There was in Virginia little of that healthful social and political contact which did so much to develop civilization at the North. Of town life there was practically nothing. Even so late as 1716 Jamestown had only a sorry half-dozen structures, two of which

Captain John Smith.

were church and court-house. Fifteen years later Fredericksburg had, besides the manor house of Colonel Willis and its belongings, only a store, a tailor shop, a blacksmith shop, a tavern or "ordinary," and a coffeehouse. Richmond and Petersburg still existed only on paper, and if we come down to the middle of the eighteenth century, Williamsburg, the capital of the province, was nothing but a straggling village of two hundred houses, without a single paved street. Only the College and the governor's "palace" were of brick. The county-seats were mostly mere glades in the woods, containing each its court-house, prison, whipping-post, pillory, and ducking-stool, besides the wretched tavern where court and attendants put up, and possibly a church. Hardships and dissensions marked the whole early history of this infant state. At one time only forty settlers remained alive, at another meal and water were the sole diet. Hoping for instant riches in gold, poor gentlemen and vagabonds had come, too much to the exclusion of mechanics and laborers. For relief from the turbulence and external dangers of this period, the colony owed much to Captain John Smith, who, after all allowance for his boasting, certainly displayed great courage and energy in emergencies. He, too, it was who did most to explore the

Pocahontas saving Captain Smith's Life.

From Smith's "General History."

country up the James and upon Chesapeake Bay.

A new charter was granted in 1609, the

council in England being now appointed by the stockholders instead of the king, and the governor of the colony being named by this council. Lord Delaware was made Governor and Captain-General of Virginia, and many more colonists sent out. By a wreck of two of the vessels there was delay in the arrival of the newly chosen officers. Smith, then Percy, meantime continued to exercise authority. This, again, was a critical period. Indians were troublesome. Tillage having been neglected from the first, provisions became exhausted, and a crisis long referred to as "the starving time" ensued. The colony had actually abandoned Jamestown and shipped for England, when met in James River by Lord Delaware, coming with relief. They at once returned, and an era of hope dawned. This was in June, 1610. One hundred and fifty new settlers accompanied Delaware. Planting was vigorously prosecuted, the Indians placated, and still further accessions of people and cattle secured from England.

Delaware's brief, mild sway was always a benediction, in pleasing contrast with the severities of Dale and Argall, who successively governed after his departure. Under Dale, death was the penalty for slaughtering cattle, even one's own, except with the Governor's leave, also of exporting goods without permission. A baker giving short weight was to lose his ears, and on second repetition to suffer death. A laundress purloining linen was to be flogged. Martial law alone prevailed; even capital punishment was ordained without jury. Such arbitrary rule was perhaps necessary, so lawless were the mass of the population. It at any rate had the excellent effect of rousing the Virginians to political thought and to the assertion of their rights. In 1612 a change took place in the Company's methods of governing its colony. The superior council was abolished, its authority transferred to the corporation as a whole, which met as an assembly to elect officers and enact laws for the colony. The government thus became more democratic in form and spirit.

The year 1614 was distinguished by the marriage of Pocahontas, daughter of the native chief Powhatan, to the English colo-

The Council of Powhatan

From Smith's "General History."

nist Rolfe. With him she visited England, dying there a few years later. The alliance secured the valuable friendship of Powhatan and his subjects—only till Powhatan's death, however. Thenceforth savage hostilities occurred at frequent intervals. In 1622 they were peculiarly severe, over three hundred settlers losing their lives through them. Another outbreak took place about 1650, this time more quickly suppressed. We shall see in a later chapter how Bacon's Rebellion was occasioned by Indian troubles.

As James I. broke with Parliament, a majority of the Virginia shareholders proved Liberals, and they wrought with signal purpose and effect to realize their ideas in their colony. To this political complexion of the Virginia Company not only Virginia itself, but, in a way, all America is indebted for a start toward free institutions. During the governorship of George Yeardley, was summoned an assembly of burgesses, consisting of two representatives, elected by the inhabitants, from each of the eleven boroughs or districts which the colony had by this time come to embrace. It met on June 30, 1619, the earliest legislative body in the New World. This was the dawn of another new era in the colony's history.

In 1622 arrived Sir Thomas Wyatt, bringing a written constitution from the Com-

Pocahontas.

pany, which confirmed to the colony representative government and trial by jury. The assembly was given authority to make laws, subject only to the Governor's veto. This enlargement of political rights was due to the growth of the sentiment of popular liberty in England. In the meetings of the London Company debates were frequent and spirited between the court faction and the supporters of the political rights of the colonists. James I., dissatisfied with the authority which he had himself granted, appointed a commission to inquire into the Company's management, and also into the circumstances of the colony. A change was recommended, the courts decided as the king wished, and the Company was dissolved. The colony, while still allowed to govern itself by means of its popular assembly, was thus brought directly under the supervision of the Crown. Charles I., coming to the throne in 1625, gave heed to the affairs of the colony only so far as necessary to secure for himself the profits of the tobacco trade. It was doubtless owing to his indifference that the colony continued to enjoy civil freedom. He again appointed Yeardley Governor, a choice agreeable to the people; and in 1628, by asking that the assembly be called in order to vote him a monopoly of the coveted trade, he explicitly recognized the legitimacy and authority of that body.

Yeardley was succeeded by Harvey, who rendered himself unpopular by defending in all land disputes the claims arising under royal grant against those based upon occupancy. Difficulties of this sort pervaded all colonial history.

In 1639 Wyatt held the office, succeeded in 1642 by Berkeley, during whose administration the colony attained its highest prosperity. Virginians now possessed constitutional rights and privileges in even a higher degree than Englishmen in the northern colonies. The colonists were most loyal to the king, and were let alone. They were also attached to the Church of England, ever manifesting toward those of a different faith the spirit of intolerance characteristic of the age.

During the civil war in England, Virginia, of course, sided with the king. When Cromwell had assumed the reins of government he sent an expedition to require the submission of the colony. An agreement was made by which the authority of Parliament was acknowledged, while the colony in return was left unmolested in the management of its own affairs.

William Berkeley

Signature of Berkeley.

CHAPTER V.

PILGRIM AND PURITAN AT THE NORTH

THE Pilgrims who settled New England were Independents, peculiar in their ecclesiastical tenet that the single congregation of godly persons, however few or humble, regularly organized for Christ's work, is of right, by divine appointment, the highest ecclesiastical authority on earth. A church of this order existed in London by 1568; another, possibly more than one, the "Brownists," by 1580. Barrowe and Greenwood began a third in 1588, which, its founders being executed, went exiled to Amsterdam in 1593, subsequently uniting with the Presbyterians there. These churches, though independent, were not strictly democratic, like those next to be named.

Soon after 1600 John Smyth gathered a

church at Gainsborough in Lincolnshire, England, which persecution likewise drove to Amsterdam. Here Smyth seceded and founded a Baptist church, which, returning to London in 1611 or 1612, became the first church of its kind known to have existed in

Plymouth Harbor, England.

England. From Smyth's church at Gainsborough sprang one at Scrooby, in Nottinghamshire, and this, too, exiled like its parent, crossed to Holland, finding home in Leyden in 1607 and 1608. Of this church John Robinson was pastor, and from its bosom came the Plymouth Colony to New England.

This little band set out for America with a patent from the Virginia Company, according to James I.'s charter of 1606, but actually began here as labor-share holders

Harbor of Provincetown, Cape Cod, where the Pilgrims andeo.

in a sub-corporation of a new organization, the Plymouth Company, chartered in 1620. Launching in the Mayflower from Plymouth, where they had paused in their way hither from Holland, they arrived off the coast of Cape Cod in 1620, December 11th Old Style, December 21st New Style, and began a settlement, to which they gave the name Plymouth. Before landing they had

The Life of the Colony at Cape Cod.

formed themselves into a political body, a government of the people with "just and equal laws."

They based their civil authority upon this Mayflower compact, practically ignoring England. Carver was the first governor, Bradford the second. The colony was named Plymouth in memory of hospitalities which its members had received at Plymouth, England, the name having no connection with the "Plymouth" of the Plymouth Company. The members of the Plymouth Company had none but a mercantile interest in the adventure, merely fitting out the colonists and bearing the expense of the passage for all but the first. On the other hand, the stock was not all retained in England. Shares were allotted to the Pilgrims as well, one to each emigrant with or without means, and one for every £10 invested.

Plymouth early made a treaty with Massasoit, the chief of the neighboring Wampanoags, the peace lasting with benign effects to both parties for fifty years, or till the outbreak of Philip's War, discussed in a later chapter. The first winter in Plymouth was one of dreadful hardships, of famine, disease and death, which spring relieved but in part. Yet Plymouth grew, surely if slowly. It acquired rights on the Kenne-

In witnes whereof the said President & Counsell haue to the one p͠t of this p͠nte Indenture sett their seales* And to th'otner p͠t hereof the said John Peirce in the name of himself and his said Associat{ haue sett to his seale geven the day and yeeres first aboue written/

Signatures to Plymouth Patent.

bec, on the Connecticut, at Cape Ann. It was at first a pure democracy, its laws all made in mass-meetings of the entire body of male inhabitants; nor was it till 1639 that increase of numbers forced resort to the principle of representation. In 1643 the population was about three thousand.

Between 1620 and 1630 there were isolated settlers along the whole New England coast. White, a minister from Dorchester, England, founded a colony near Cape Ann, which removed to Salem in 1626. The Plymouth Company granted them a patent, which Endicott, in charge of more emi

Site of First Church and Governor Bradford's House at Plymouth.

grants, brought over in 1628. It gave title to all land between the Merrimac and Charles Rivers, also to all within three miles beyond each. These men formed the nucleus of the colony to which in 1629 Charles I. granted a royal charter, styling the proprietors "the Governor and Company of the Massachusetts Bay in New England." Boston was made the capital. Soon more emigrants came, and Charlestown was settled.

It was a momentous step when the government of this colony was transferred to New England. Winthrop was chosen Governor, others of the Company elected to minor offices, and they, with no fewer than one thousand new colonists, sailed for this side the Atlantic. In Massachusetts, therefore, a trading company did not *beget*, as elsewhere, but literally *became* a political state. Many of the Massachusetts men, in contrast with those of Plymouth, had enjoyed high consideration at home. Yet democracy prevailed here too. The Governor and his eighteen assistants were chosen

by the freemen, and were both legislature
and court. As population increased and
scattered in towns, these chose deputies to
represent them, and a lower house element
was added to the General Court, though

Governor Winthrop.

assistants and deputies did not sit sepa-
rately till 1644. At this time Massachusetts had a population of about 15,000. To
all New England 21,200 emigrants came
between 1628 and 1643, the total white

population at the latter date being about 24,000.

So early as 1631 this colony decreed to admit none as freemen who were not also church members. Thus Church and State were made one, the government a theoc-

First Church in Salem.

racy. The Massachusetts settlers, though in many things less extreme than the Pilgrims, were decided Puritans, sincere but formal, precise, narrow, and very superstitious. They did not, however, on coming hither, affect or wish to separate from the Church of England, earnestly as they deprecated retaining the sign of the cross in baptism, the surplice, marriage with ring, and kneeling at communion. Yet soon they in effect became Separatists as well as Puritans, building independent churches, like those at Plymouth, and repudiating episcopacy utterly.

Much as these Puritans professed and tried to exalt reason in certain matters, in civil

Seal of Massachusetts Bay Company.

and religious affairs, where they took the Old Testament as affording literal and minute directions for all sorts of human actions for all time, they could allow little liberty of opinion. This was apparent when into this theocratic state came Roger Williams, afterward the founder of Rhode Island. Born in London, England, about 1607, of good family, he was placed by his patron, Coke, at the Charter House School.

From there he went to Pembroke College, Cambridge. In 1631 he arrived in Boston. Somewhat finical in his political, moral, and religious ideas, he found it impossible, having separated from the Church of England, in which he had been reared, to harmonize here with those still favoring that communion. At Salem he was invited by a little company of Separatists to become their teacher. His views soon offended the authorities. He declared that the king's patent could confer no title to lands possessed by Indians. He denied the right of magistrates to punish heresy, or to enforce attendance upon religious services. "The magistrate's power," he said, "extends only to the bodies, goods, and outward state of men."

Alarmed at his bold utterances, the General Court of Massachusetts, September 2, 1635, decreed his banishment for "new and dangerous opinions, against the authority of magistrates." His fate was not, therefore, merely because of his religious views. The exile sought refuge at Seekonk, but this being within the Plymouth jurisdiction, he, on Governor Winslow's admonition, moved farther into the wilderness, settling at Providence. He purchased land of the natives, and, joined by others, set up a pure democracy, instituting as a part thereof the "lively experiment," for which ages had waited, of

Roger Williams' House at Salem.

perfect liberty in matters of religious belief. Not for the first time in history, but more clearly, earnestly, and consistently than it had ever been done before, he maintained for every man the right of absolute freedom in matters of conscience, for all forms of faith equal toleration.

Some friends of Mrs. Anne Hutchinson

established a colony on Aquidneck, the Indian name for Rhode Island. Williams went to England and secured from Parliament a patent which united that plantation with his in one government. Charles II.'s charter of 1663 added Warwick to the first two settlements, renewing and enlarging the

Edward Winslow.

patent, and giving freest scope for government according to Williams' ideas. Mrs. Hutchinson, a woman of rare intellect and eloquence, who maintained the right of private judgment and pretended to an infallible inner light of revelation, was, like Williams, a victim of Puritan intolerance.

She and her followers were banished, and some of them, returning, put to death, 1659-60. She came to Providence, then went to Aquidneck, where her husband died in 1642. She next settled near Hurl Gate, within the Dutch limits, where herself and almost her entire family were butchered by the Indians in 1643.

In 1633 the Dutch erected a fort where Hartford now is, but some English emigrants from Plymouth Colony, in defiance of a threatened cannonade, sailed past and built a trading-house at Windsor, where, joined by colonists, from about Boston, they soon effected a settlement. Wethersfield and Hartford were presently founded. In 1630 the Plymouth Company had granted Connecticut to the Earl of Warwick, who turned it over to Lord Brooke, Lord Say-and-Seal, and others. Winthrop the Younger, son of Governor Winthrop, of Massachusetts, commissioned by these last, built a fort at Saybrook. Till the expiration of his commission the towns immediately upon the Connecticut were under the government of

Massachusetts. Their population in 1643 was three thousand. A convention of these towns met at Hartford, January 14, 1639, and formed a constitution, like that of Massachusetts Bay, thoroughly republican in nature. Connecticut breathed a freer spirit than either Massachusetts or New Haven, being in this respect the peer of Plymouth. At Hartford Roger Williams was always welcome.

Meantime, in 1638, having touched at Boston the year before, Davenport, Eaton, and others from London began planting at New Haven. The Bible was adopted as their guide in both civil and religious affairs, and a government organized in which only church members could vote or be elected to the General Court. The colony flourished, branching out into several towns. In 1643 it numbered twenty-five hundred inhabitants.

As early as 1622, Mason and Gorges were granted land partly in what is now Maine, partly in what is now New Hampshire; and in 1623 Dover and Portsmouth were settled. Wheelwright, a brother-in-law of Mrs. Hutchinson, with others, purchased of the natives the southeast part of New Hampshire, between the Merrimac and the Piscataqua, and in 1638 Exeter was founded. In the same year with Wheelwright's purchase, Mason obtained from the council of the Plymouth Company a patent to this same section, and the tract was called New Hampshire. These conflicting claims paved the way for future controversies and lawsuits. The settlers here were not Puritans, nor were they obliged to be church members in order to be deputies or freemen.

The settlement of Maine goes back to 1626, when the Plymouth Company granted lands there both to Alexander and to Gorges. In 1639 Gorges secured a royal charter to re-enforce his claim. Large freedom, civil and religious, was allowed. For many years the Maine settlements were small and scattered, made up mostly of such as came to hunt and fish for a season only.

From 1643 to 1684 Massachusetts, Plymouth, Connecticut, and New Haven formed a confederation under the style of the United Colonies of New England. Maine, Providence, and Rhode Island sought membership, but were refused as being civilly and religiously out of harmony with the colonies named. Connecticut, offensive to the Dutch, and exposed to hostilities from them, was the most earnest for the union, while at the same time the most conservative as to its form. It was a loose league, leaving each colony independent save as to war and peace, Indian affairs, alliances and boundaries. Questions pertaining to these were to be settled by a commission of two delegates from each of the four colonies, meeting yearly, voting man by man, six out of the eight votes being necessary to bind.

The confederacy settled a boundary dispute between New Haven and New Netherland in 1650. It received and disbursed moneys, amounting some years to £600, for the propagation of the gospel in New

England, sent over by the society which Parliament incorporated for that purpose in 1649. It was also of more or less service in securing united action against the savages in Philip's War. The union was, however, of little immediate service, useful rather as an example for the far future. Its failure was due partly to the distance of the colonies apart, and to the strength of the instinct for local self-government, a distinguishing political trait of New England till our day. Its main weakness, however, was the overbearing power and manner of Massachusetts, especially after her assumption of Maine in 1652. In 1653 the Plymouth, New Haven, and Connecticut commissioners earnestly wished war with New Netherland, but Massachusetts proudly forbade—a plain violation of the articles. After this there was not much heart in the alliance. The last meeting of the commissioners occurred at Hartford, September 5, 1684.

CHAPTER VI.

BALTIMORE AND HIS MARYLAND

THF very year that witnessed the landing of the Pilgrims records the beginning of another attempt to colonize the New World. While Secretary of State, having been appointed in 1619, Sir George Calvert, a member of the Virginia Company from 1609 until its dissolution in 1624, determined to plant a colony for himself. In the memorable year 1620 he bought of Lord Vaughan the patent to the southeastern peninsula of Newfoundland, the next he sent colonists thither with a generous supply of money for their support. In

Maryland Shilling.

1623 King James gave him a patent, making him proprietary of this region. In 1625 Calvert boldly declared himself a Catholic, and resigned his office of Secretary. Spite of this he was soon afterwards ennobled, and his new title of Lord Baltimore is the name by which he is best known. Visiting his little settlement in 1627 he quickly came to the conclusion that the severity of the climate would make its failure certain. He therefore gave up this enterprise, but determined to repeat the attempt on the more favorable soil of Virginia. Confident of the goodwill of Charles I., to whom he had written for a grant of land there, he did not await a reply, but sailed for Virginia, where he arrived in 1629. In 1632 the king issued a patent granting to Baltimore and his heirs a territory north and east of the Potomac, comprising what we now call Maryland, all Delaware, and a part of Pennsylvania. The name Maryland was given it by the king in honor of his queen, Henrietta Maria. But before this charter had received royal signature Lord Baltimore had breathed his last, and his son Cecil succeeded to his honors and possessions.

The Maryland charter made the proprietary the absolute lord of the soil. He was merely to acknowledge fealty by the delivery of two Indian arrows yearly to the king at Windsor. He could make laws with the

Henrietta Maria.

consent of the citizens, declare war or peace, appoint officers of government; in fact, in most respects he had regal power. The colonists were, however, to remain English subjects, with all the privileges of such. If they were not represented in Parliament, neither were they taxed by the Crown. If the proprietary made laws for them, these must not be contrary to the laws of England. And they were to enjoy freedom of trade, not only with England but with foreign countries.

This charter, as will be readily seen, could not please the Virginians, since the entire territory conveyed by it was part of the grant of 1609 to the London Company for Virginia. But as this and subsequent charters had been annulled in 1624, the new colony was held by the Privy Council to have the law on its side, and Lord Baltimore was left to make his preparations undisturbed. He fitted out two vessels, the Ark and the Dove, and sent them on their voyage of colonization. They went by the way of the West Indies, arriving off Point Comfort in 1634. Sailing up the Potomac, they landed on the island of St. Clement's, and took formal possession of their new home. Calvert explored a river, now called the St. Mary's, a tributary of the Potomac, and being pleased with the spot began a settlement. He gained the friendship of the natives by purchasing the land and by treating them justly and humanely.

The proprietary was a Catholic, yet, whether or not by an agreement between

Supposed Portrait of William Clayborne.

him and the king, as Gardiner supposes, did not use either his influence or his authority to distress adherents of the Church of England. The two creeds stood practically upon an equality. But if religious troubles were avoided, difficulties of another sort were not slow in arising. About the year 1631, Clayborne, who had been secretary of the Virginia colony, had chosen Kent Island in Chesapeake Bay as a station for

Clayborne's Trading Post on Kent Island.

trading with the Indians. This post was in the very midst of Maryland, and Calvert notified Clayborne that he should consider it a part of that province. Clayborne at once showed himself a bitter enemy. The Indians became suspicious and unfriendly, Clayborne, so it was believed, being the instigator of this temper. An armed vessel was sent out, with orders from Clayborne to seize ships of the St. Mary's settlement. A fight took place, Clayborne fleeing to Virginia. Calvert demanded that he should be given up. This was refused, and in 1637 he went to England. A committee of the Privy Council decided that Kent Island belonged to Maryland.

In 1635 the first Maryland assembly met, consisting of the freemen of the colony and the governor, Leonard Calvert, the proprietary's brother, who was presiding officer. Lord Baltimore repudiated its acts, on the ground that they were not proposed by him, as the charter directed. The assembly which gathered in 1638 retaliated, rejecting the laws brought forward by the proprietary.

For a time the colony was without laws except the common law of England. But Baltimore was too wise and conciliatory to allow such a state of affairs to continue. He gave authority to the governor to assent to the acts of the assembly, which he himself might or might not confirm.

Accordingly in 1639 the assembly met and passed various acts, mostly relating to civil

Fight between Clayborne and the St. Mary's Ship.

affairs. One, however, was specially noteworthy, as giving to the "Holy Church" "her rights and liberties," meaning by this the Church of Rome, for, as Gardiner says, the title was never applied to the Church of England. It was at the same time expressly enacted that all the Christian inhabitants should be in the enjoyment of every right and privilege as free as the natural-born subjects of England. If Roger Williams was the first to proclaim absolute religious liberty, Lord Baltimore was hardly behind him in putting this into practice. As has been neatly said, "The Ark and the Dove were names of happy omen: the one saved from the general wreck the germs of political liberty, and the other bore the olive-branch of religious peace."

During the civil war in England th affairs of Maryland were in a very disturbed condition. Clayborne, Maryland's evil genius, seized the opportunity to foment an insurrection, possessed himself once more of Kent Island, and compelled the governor to flee to Virginia. Returning in 1646, Calvert was fortunate enough to recover the reins of government, but the following year witnessed the close of his administra tion and his short though useful and eventful life. Few men intrusted with almost absolute authority have exercised it with so much firmness and at the same time with so much ability, discretion, and uprightness.

His successor, Greene, a Catholic, was not likely to find favor with the Puritan Parliament of England. and Baltimore, in 1648, to conciliate the ruling powers and to refute the charge that Maryland was only a retreat for Romanists, removed the governor and appointed instead one who was a Protestant and a firm supporter of Parliament. The council was also changed so as to place the Catholics in the minority. The oath of the new governor restrained him from molesting any person, especially if of the Roman Catholic persuasion, on account of religious profession. The way was thus opened for the Act of Toleration passed in 1649. This law, after specifying certain peeches against the Trinity, the Virgin, or the saints as punishable offences, declared that equal privileges should be enjoyed by Christians of all creeds. Whatever the motives of Baltimore, his policy was certainly wise and commendable.

A new and troublesome element was now introduced into the colony. Some Puritans who had not been tolerated among the stanch Church-of-England inhabitants of Virginia were invited by Governor Stone to Maryland. Their home here, which they named Providence, is now known as Annapolis. The new-comers objected to the oath of fidelity, refused to send burgesses to the assembly, and were ready to overthrow the government whose protection they were enjoying. Opportunity soon offered. Parliament had already in 1652 brought Virginia to submission. Maryland was now accused of disloyalty, and when we notice among the commissioners appointed by the Council of State, the name of Clayborne, it is not difficult to understand who was the author of this charge. The governor was removed, but being popular and not averse to compromise, was quickly restored. Then came the accession of Cromwell to power as Protector of England. Parliament was dissolved. The authority of its commissioners of course ceased. Baltimore seized this opportunity to regain his position as proprietary. He bade Stone to require the oath

Oliver Cromwell.

of fidelity to the proprietary from those who occupied lands, and to issue all writs in his name. He maintained that the province now stood in the same relations to the Protectorate which it had borne to the royalist government of Charles I.

So thought Cromwell, but not so Clayborne or the Maryland Puritans. They deposed Stone, and put in power Fuller, who was in sympathy with their designs. There resulted a reversal of the acts of former assemblies, and legislation hostile to the Catholics. The new assembly, from which Catholics were carefully excluded by disfranchisement, at once repealed the Act of Toleration. Protection was withdrawn from those who professed the popish religion, and they were forbidden the exercise of that faith in the province. Severe penalties were threatened against "prelacy" and "licentiousness," thus restricting the benefits of their "Act concerning Religion" to the Puritan element now in power. The authority of the proprietary himself was disputed, and colonists were invited to take lands without his knowledge or consent.

Baltimore adopted vigorous measures. By his orders Stone made a forcible attempt to regain control of the province, but was defeated at Providence and taken prisoner. His life was spared, but four of his men were condemned and executed. Baltimore again invoked the powerful intervention of Cromwell, and again were the enemies of Maryland sternly rebuked for their interference in the affairs of that province, and told in plain language to leave matters as they had found them. In 1656, after an inquiry by the Commissioners of Trade, the claims of Baltimore were admitted to be just, and he promptly sent his brother Philip to be a member of the council and secretary of the province. The legislation of the usurping Puritans was set aside, religious toleration once more had full sway, and a general pardon was proclaimed to those who had taken part in the late disturbances.

In the meantime, Fendall, who had been appointed governor by Baltimore, plotted to make himself independent of his master, and, with the connivance of the assembly, proceeded to usurp the authority which was lawfully vested in the proprietary. But the attempt was a miserable failure. Philip Calvert was immediately made governor by the now all-powerful proprietary, who had the favor and support of Charles II., just coming to the throne. Peace and prosperity came back to the colony so sorely and frequently vexed by civil dissensions. The laws were just and liberal, encouraging the advent of settlers of whatever creed, while the rule of the Calverts was wise and benign, such as to merit the respect and admiration of posterity. In 1643 Virginia and Maryland together had less than twenty thousand inhabitants. In 1660 Maryland alone, according to Fuller, had eight thousand. Chalmers thinks there were no fewer than twelve thousand at this date.

CHAPTER VII.

NEW NETHERLAND

WHILE the French explorer, Champlain, was sailing along the shores of the lake which bears his name, another equally adventurous spirit, Henry Hudson, was on his way to the western world. Hoping to open a passage to India by a voyage to the north, Hudson, an English navigator, offered in 1609 to sail under the authority of the Dutch East India Company. Driven back by ice and fog from a northeast course, he turned northwest. Searching up and down near the parallel of 40°, he entered the mouth of the great river which perpetuates his name. He found the country inviting to the eye, and occupied by natives friendly in disposition. The subsequent career of this bold mariner has a mournful interest. He never returned to

Holland, but, touching at Dartmouth, was restrained by the English authorities, and forbidden longer to employ his skill and experience for the benefit of the Dutch. Again entering the English service and sent once more to discover the northwest passage, he sailed into the waters of the bay

Seal of New Amsterdam.

which still bears his name, where cold and hunger transformed the silent discontent of his crew into open mutiny, and they left the fearless navigator to perish amid the icebergs of the frozen north.

Hudson had sent to Holland a report of the Great River and the country bordering

Peter Stuyvesant.

it, rich in fur-bearing animals, and it had excited eager interest. Private individuals sent expeditions thither and carried on a profitable trade with the natives. A few Dutch were here when, in 1613, Captain Argall sailed from Virginia against the French at Port Royal, Acadia, now Annapolis in Nova Scotia, who were encroaching upon the English possessions on the coast of Maine. He compelled them to surrender. On his return, he visited the Dutch traders of Manhattan Island, and forced them also, as it had been discovered by Cabot in 1497, to acknowledge the sovereignty of England over this entire region.

It was in 1614 that the Dutch States-General, in the charter given to a company of merchants, named the Hudson Valley New Netherland. To facilitate trade this company made a treaty with the Five Nations and subordinate tribes,

Seal of New Netherland.

memorable as the first compact formed between the whites and the savages. In it the Indians were regarded as possessing equal rights and privileges with their white brethren. The treaty was renewed in 1645, and continued in force till the English occupation, 1664. In 1618, the charter of the New Netherland Company having expired, the Dutch West India Company was offered a limited incorporation, but it was not until 1621 that it received its charter, and it was two years later that it was completely organized and approved by the States-General. By this company were sent out Mey, as Director, to the Delaware or South River, and Tienpont to the Hudson or North River. Four miles below Philadelphia Fort Nassau was erected, and where Albany now stands was begun the trading-post called Fort Orange.

In 1626 Tienpont's successor, Peter Minuit, a German, born at Wesel, was appointed Director-General of New Netherland. He bought of the Indians, for the sum of twenty-four dollars, the entire island of Manhattan, and a fort called New Amsterdam was built. The State of New York dates its beginning from this transaction.

By their usually honest dealing with the natives the Dutch settlers gained the

Earliest Picture of New Amsterdam.

friendship of the Five Nations, whose good-will was partly on this account transferred to the English colonists later. The Dutch were not only friendly to the red men, but tried to open social and commercial relations with the Plymouth colonists as well. Governor Bradford replied, mildly urging the Dutch to "clear their title" to a territory which the English claimed by right of discovery.

The present State of Delaware soon

De Vries.

became the scene of attempts at settlement. De Vries began, in 1632, a colony on the banks of the Delaware, but it was quickly laid waste by the savages, who had been needlessly provoked by the insolence of the commander left in charge of the colony. In 1633 Minuit was succeeded by Van Twiller, and a fort was erected at

Hartford, though the English claimed this country as theirs. Emigrants from the Plymouth colony began the settlement of Windsor, in spite of the protests of the Dutch. Long Island was invaded by enterprising New Englanders, regardless of the claim of New Netherland thereto.

This "irrepressible conflict" between two races was by no means abated by the introduction of a third. As early as 1626, Gus-

Costumes of Swedes.

tavus Adolphus, King of Sweden and the hero of the Thirty Years' War, had entertained the idea of establishing colonies in America, and in pursuance of that object had encouraged the formation of a company, not only for trading purposes but also to secure a refuge for the "oppressed of all Christendom." To Usselinx, an Antwerp merchant, the originator of the Dutch West India Company, belongs the honor of first suggesting to the king this enterprise. The glorious death of Gustavus on the victorious field of Lützen in 1632 deferred the execution of a purpose which had not been forgotten even in the midst of that long and arduous campaign. But a few days before he fell, the Protestant hero had spoken of the colonial prospect as "the jewel of his kingdom."

In 1638 Minuit, who had already figured as governor of New Netherland, having offered his services to Sweden, was intrusted with the leadership of the first Swedish colony to America. After a few days' stay at Jamestown the new-comers finally reached their wished-for destination on the west shore of the Delaware Bay and River. Proceeding up the latter, one of their first acts was to build a fort on a little stream about two miles from its junction with the Delaware, which they named Fort Christina, in honor of the young queen of Sweden. Near this spot stands the present city of Wilmington. The country from Cape Henlopen to the falls at Trenton received the title of New Sweden.

It was in this very year that Kieft came to supersede Van Twiller, who had given just cause for complaint by his eagerness to enrich himself at the expense of the West India Company. During the administration of Kieft occurred the long and doubtful conflict with the natives detailed in the succeeding chapter. Arbitrary and exacting, he drove the Indians to extremities, and involved the Dutch settlements in a war which for a time threatened their destruction. Not till 1645 was peace re-established, and in 1647 the unpopular governor was recalled. In 1647 not more than three hundred fighting men remained in the whole province. Its total population was between fifteen hundred and two thousand. In 1652 New Amsterdam had a population of seven or eight hundred. In 1664 Stuyvesant put the number in the province at ten thousand, about fifteen hundred of whom were in New Amsterdam.

The old Stadt Huys at New Amsterdam.

The next governor, Stuyvesant, was the last and much the ablest ruler among those who directed the destinies of New Netherland. His administration embraced a period

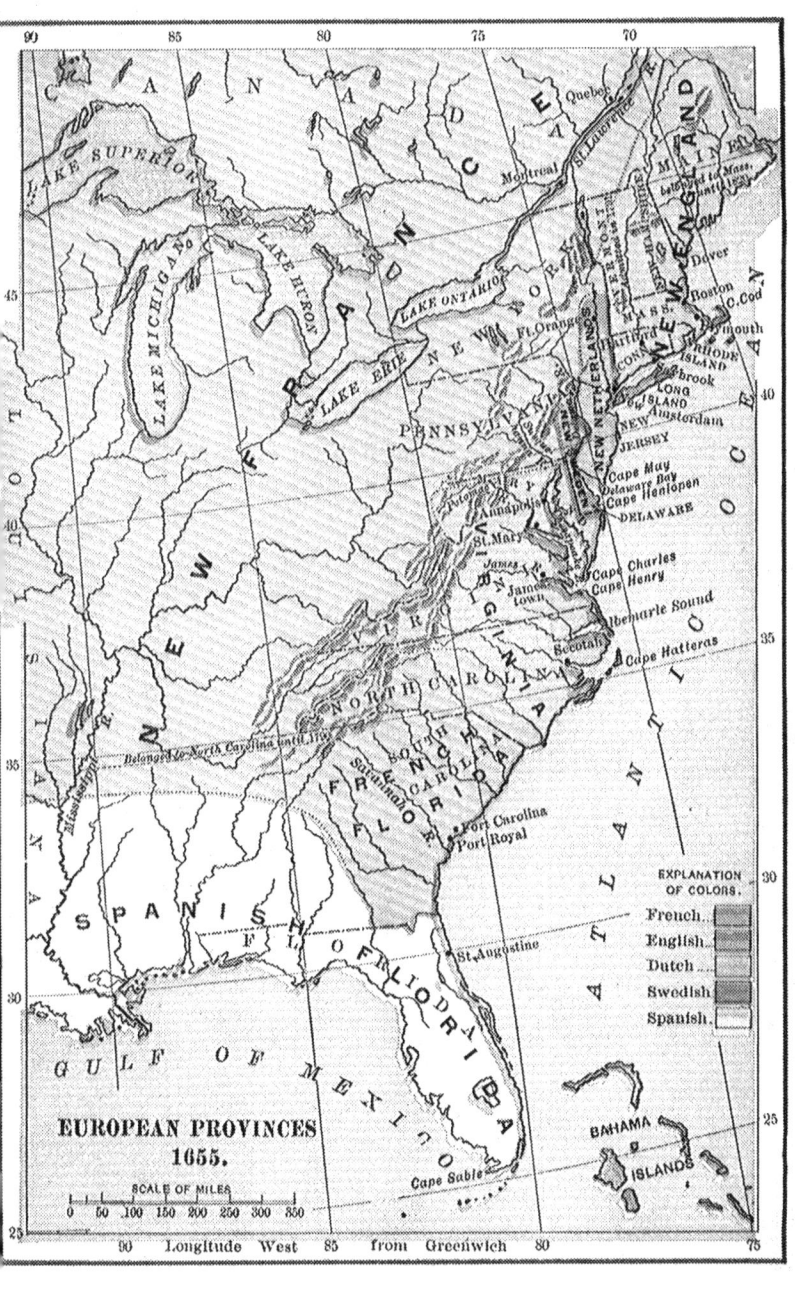

of seventeen years, during which he renewed the former friendly relations with the savages, made a treaty with New England, giving up pretensions to Connecticut as well as relinquishing the east end of Long Island, and compelled the Swedes, in 1655, to acknowledge the Dutch supremacy. It was while he was absent on his expedition against the Swedes, leaving New Amsterdam unprotected, that the river Indians, watchful of their opportunity, invaded and laid

New Amsterdam in the middle of the Seventeenth Century.

waste the surrounding country. In 1663 the savages attacked the village on the

The Duke of York, afterwards James II.

Esopus, now Kingston, and almost destroyed it. It was not until the energetic governor made a vigorous campaign against the Esopus tribe, whom he completely subdued, that peace was established on a firm footing.

But the Dutch sway in their little part of the New World was about to end. The

English had never given over their claim to the country by virtue of their first discovery of the North American continent. The New Netherlanders, tired of arbitrary rule, sighed for the larger freedom of their New England neighbors. Therefore, when in 1664 Charles II. granted to his brother, the Duke of York, the territory which the Dutch were occupying, and sent a fleet to demand its submission, the English invader

The Tomb of Stuyvesant.

was welcomed. Almost the only resistance came from the stout-hearted governor, who could hardly be dissuaded from fighting the English single-handed, and who signed the agreement to surrender only when his magistrates had, in spite of him, agreed to the proposed terms. But the founders of the Empire State have left an indelible impress upon the Union, which their descendants have helped to strengthen and perpetuate. They were honest, thrifty, devout, tolerant of the opinions of others. As Holland sheltered the English Puritans from ecclesiastical intolerance, so New Netherland welcomed within her borders the victims of New England bigotry and narrowness.

CHAPTER VIII.

THE FIRST INDIAN WARS

TROUBLES between the Indians and the whites arose so early as 1636. John Oldham was murdered on Block Island by a party of Pequot Indians. Vane of Massachusetts sent Endicott to inflict punishment. The Pequots in turn attacked the fort at Saybrook, and in 1637 threatened Wethersfield. They were planning a union with the Narragansets for the destruction of the English, when Roger Williams informed the Massachusetts colony of their designs and, at the urgent request of the governor and council, hastened to the chief of the Narragansets and dissuaded him from entering into the alliance.

The moment was critical. Captain Mason with about ninety English and seventy Mohegans, under their sachem, Uncas (a sub chief, who with his district, Mohegan, had rebelled against the Pequot sachem, Sassacus), was sent from Hartford down the Connecticut River. Entering the Sound, he sailed past the mouth of the Thames and anchored in Narragansett Bay, at the foot of Tower Hill, near Point Judith. He knew that keen-eyed scouts from the Pequot stronghold on the west bank of the Mystic River, near Groton, had, as his three little ships skirted the shore, been watching him, to give warning of his approach. He therefore resolved to come upon the enemy from an unlooked-for quarter. This plan was directly contrary to his instructions, which required him to land at the mouth of the Thames and attack the fort from the west side. He hoped, marching westward across the country, to take the enemy by surprise on their unprotected rear, while the Indians, trusting in the strength of their fort, as it fronted the west, should believe themselves secure.

Thirteen men had been sent back to the Thames with the vessels. Two hundred

Attack on

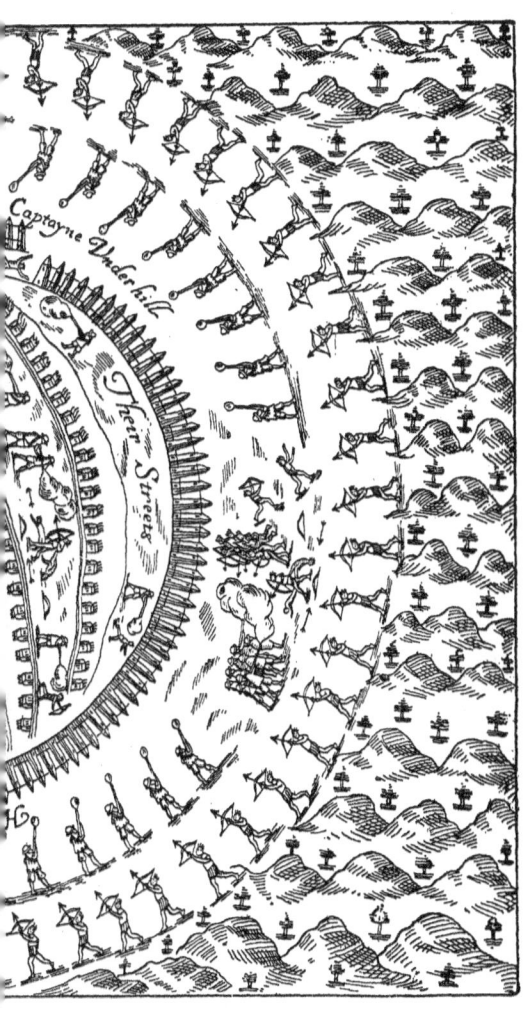

equots on the Mystic River.

Narragansets had joined the expedition, though their sachem, Miantonomoh, thought the English too weak to fight the dreaded Pequots. Mason's enterprise was admirably planned, and he was as fortunate as he was bold and skilful. He divided his men into two parties. One, led by Underhill, climbed the steep ascent on the south side of the Indian village; the other, directed by Mason himself, mounted the northern slope. The garrison was buried in slumber, made more profound by carousals the preceding night. One Indian was heard to cry out "Englishmen" before the volley of musketry from the attacking force told that the white enemy had come. Mason entered a wigwam and fought, as did the others, hand-to-hand with the now awakened and desperate foe. Coming out with a firebrand and exclaiming "We must burn them," he set fire to the wigwam. The flames were quickly carried through the fort by the northeast wind. Underhill from his side applied powder. So rapidly did the flames spread that the English had difficulty in making good their escape, while the Pequots who escaped the sword were doomed to perish by fire. In an hour's time from four hundred to six hundred had fallen, more than half of them women and children. Of the Englishmen two were killed and about twenty wounded. In this dreadful slaughter the Narragansets had little share, for they had shown such

Attack on the Pequot Fort.

fear that Mason had said to Uncas, "Tell them not to fly, but stand at what distance they please and see whether Englishmen will now fight or not."

With the approach of day three hundred Pequots advanced from a second fort intending to fight, but they were struck with horror at the sight of their dead fellow-warriors. Keeping the enemy at bay, the English marched to the vessels, which had arrived at Pequot Harbor, and, placing the wounded on board, continued their march to Saybrook. The remnant of the Pequots sought to escape from the country, moving westward along the Sound. Captain Stoughton, sent with one hundred and twenty Massachusetts men, was guided by the Narragansets to a swamp in which a little band of those hostile savages had hidden. The men were slain, offering little resistance. The women and children were divided among the Indian allies or sold into slavery by the colonists of Massachusetts Bay.

Mason and Stoughton together sailed

from Saybrook along the shore, while Uncas with his men tracked the fugitives by land. At Guilford a Pequot sachem was entrapped, shot, and his head thrust into the crotch of an oak-tree near the harbor, giving the place the name of Sachem's Head. Near the town of Fairfield a last stand was made by the hunted redskins, in a swamp, to which the English were guided by a renegade Pequot. The tribe with whom the Pequots had taken shelter, also the women and children, were allowed to give themselves up. The men were shot down or broke through and escaped. The wife of Mononotto fell into the hands of the English. This Indian squaw had once shown kindness to two captive girls, and by Winthrop's orders she was kindly treated in return. The Pequots, once so powerful, were well-nigh exterminated. Those taken prisoners were spared only to be held in bondage, Mononotto's wife with the rest. Some were absorbed by the Narragansets, others by the Mohegans, while the settlers of Connecticut, upon whom the war had fallen so heavily, came into possession of the Pequot land.

For nearly forty years the New England colonies were not again molested, the merciless vigor with which they had fought making a lasting impression upon their blood-thirsty foes. The cruel slavery to which the surviving natives were subjected, the English justified by the example of the Jews in their treatment of the Canaanites.

The Narraganset chief, Miantonomoh, had become the friend and ally of the English by a treaty ratified in 1636, mainly through the good offices of Roger Williams.

Signature of Miantonomoh.

In 1638, after the destruction of the Pequots, there was a new treaty, embracing Uncas with his bold Mohegans, and stipulating that any quarrel between Miantonomoh and Uncas should be referred to the English. In 1642 Miantonomoh was accused of plotting against the English, and summoned before the General Court at Boston. Though acquitted he vowed revenge upon Uncas as the instigator of the charge. His friendship for Roger Williams, as also for Samuel Gorton, the purchaser of Shawomet, or Warwick, R. I., which was claimed by Massachusetts, had perhaps created a prejudice against him. At any rate, when a quarrel arose between Uncas and Sequasson, Miantonomoh's friend and ally, while the latter naturally sided with Sequasson, the sympathies of the English were with Uncas, who had aided them against the Pequots. With the consent of Connecticut and Massachusetts Miantonomoh took the field against Uncas, who had attacked Sequasson. He was defeated and taken prisoner. Carried to Hartford he was held to await the decision of the Commissioners of the United Colonies at Boston. They would not release him, yet had no valid ground for putting him to death. The case was referred to five clergymen, and they voted for his execution. For this purpose the commissioners gave orders to turn the brave warrior over to Uncas, English witnesses to be present and see that no cruelty was perpetrated. The sentence was carried into effect near Norwich. Cutting a piece of flesh from the shoulder of his murdered enemy, Uncas ate it with savage relish,

The Grave of Miantonomoh.

declaring it to be the sweetest meat he had ever tasted.

The Dutch, too, as we have to some extent seen already, felt the horrors of Indian warfare. Kieft, the Dutch director-general, a man cruel, avaricious, and obstinate, angered the red men by demanding tribute from them as their protector, while he refused them guns or ammunition. The savages replied that they had to their own cost shown kindness to the Dutch when in need of food, but would not pay tribute. Kieft attacked. Some of the Indians were killed and their crops destroyed. This roused their revengeful passions to the utmost. The Raritan savages visited the colony of De Vries, on Staten Island, with death and devastation. Reward was offered for the head of any one of the murderers. An Indian never forgot an injury. The nephew of one of the natives who twenty years before had been wantonly killed went to sell furs at Fort Amsterdam, and while there revenged his uncle's murder by the slaughter of an unoffending colonist. Spite of warlike preparations by Kieft and his assembly in 1641–42, the tribe would not give up the culprit. The following year another settler was knifed by a drunken Indian. Wampum was indeed offered in atonement, while an indignant plea was urged by the savages against the liquor traffic, which demoralized their young men and rendered them dangerous alike to friend and foe. But remonstrance and blood-money could not satisfy Kieft. At Pavonia and at Corlaer's Hook[1] the Dutch fell venomously upon the sleeping and unsuspecting enemy. Men, women, and children were slaughtered, none spared. In turn the tribes along the lower Hudson, to the number of eleven, united and desperately attacked the Dutch wherever found. Only near the walls of Fort Amsterdam was there safety. The governor appointed a day of fasting, which it seems was kept with effect. The sale of liquor to the red men was at last prohibited, and peace for a time secured.

Soon, however, the redskins along the Hudson were again up in arms. The noted Underhill, who with Mason had been the scourge of the Pequots, came to the fight

[1] Now in the New York City limits, just below Broadway Ferry, East River.

with fifty Englishmen as allies of the Dutch. Not waiting to be attacked, the Indians laid waste the settlements, even threatening Fort Amsterdam itself. At a place now known as Pelham Neck, near New Rochelle, lived the famous but unfortunate Mrs. Hutchinson, a fugitive from the persecuting zeal of Massachusetts. Here the implacable savages butchered her and her family in cold blood. Her little granddaughter alone was spared, and led captive to a far-off wigwam prison. Only at Gravesend, on Long Island, was a successful stand made, and that by a woman, Lady Deborah Moody, another exile from religious persecution, who with forty stout-hearted men defended her plantation and compelled the savages to beat a retreat.

The colony was in extremity. New Haven refused to aid, because, as a member of the New England confederacy, it could not act alone, and because it was not satisfied that the Dutch war was just. An appeal was made by Kieft's eight advisers to both the States-General and the West

India Company in Holland. The sad condition of the colonists was fully set forth, and the responsibility directly ascribed to the mismanagement of Kieft. At the same time, undismayed by the gloomy outlook, the courage of the sturdy Dutchmen rose with the emergency. Small parties were sent out against the Connecticut savages in the vicinity of Stamford. Indian villages on Long Island were surprised and the natives put to the sword. In two instances at least the victors disgraced humanity by torturing the captured.

In these engagements Underhill was conspicuous and most energetic. Having made himself familiar with the position of the Indians near Stamford, he sailed from Manhattan with one hundred and fifty men, landed at Greenwich, and, marching all day, at midnight drew near the enemy. His approach was not wholly unannounced, for the moon was full. The fight was desperate and bloody. The tragedy that had made memorable the banks of the Mystic in the destruction of the Pequot fort was now almost equalled. After the example of his old comrade Mason, Underhill fired the village. By flame, shot, or sword more than five hundred human beings perished.

While New Netherland was awaiting some message of cheer from Holland, a company of Dutch soldiers came from Curaçoa, but they did little to follow up the successes already gained. Again the Eight sent a memorial to the company, boldly condemning the conduct of the director and demanding his recall. Their remonstrances were at last heeded, and the removal of the unpopular governor resolved upon. In 1647 Kieft set sail for Holland, but the ship was wrecked, and he with nearly all on board was drowned.

It was high time for a change. In the two years, 1643–45, while sixteen hundred Indians had been slain, Manhattan had become nearly depopulated. In 1645 peace was concluded, not only with the smaller tribes in the vicinity, but also with the powerful Mohawks about Fort Orange, and finally with all the Indians belonging to the Five Nations or acknowledging their authority. A pleasing incident of this treaty was the promise of the Indians to restore the eight-year-old granddaughter of Mrs. Hutchinson, a promise which they faithfully performed in 1646. The great compact was made under the shadow of the Fort Amsterdam walls, and the universal joy was expressed by a day of thanksgiving.

Totem or Tribe Mark of the Five Nations.

An interval of peace for ten years was now enjoyed, when the killing of a squaw for stealing some peaches led to an attack by several hundred of the infuriated savages upon New Amsterdam. They were repulsed here, but crossing to the shore of New Jersey they laid waste the settlements there. Staten Island, too, was swept with fire and sword. One hundred people were slain, 150 more taken captive, 300 made homeless. Peace was again effected and maintained for three years, when fresh quarrels began. It was not until 1660 that a more general and lasting treaty was brought about, on which occasion a Mohawk and a Minqua chief gave pledges in behalf of the Indians, and acted as mediators between the contending parties.

PERIOD II.

ENGLISH AMERICA TILL THE END OF THE FRENCH AND INDIAN WAR

1660-1763

CHAPTER I.

NEW ENGLAND UNDER THE LAST STUARTS

THE Commonwealth in England went to pieces at the death of Oliver Cromwell, its founder. The Stuart dynasty came back, but, alas! unimproved. Charles II. was a much meaner man than his father, and James II. was more detestable still. The rule of such kings was destined to work sad changes in the hitherto free condition of Massachusetts. This colony had sympathized with the Commonwealth more heartily than any of the others. Hither had fled for refuge Goffe and Whalley, two of the accomplices in the death of Charles I. Congregational church polity was here established by law, to the exclusion of all others, even of episcopacy, for whose sake Charles was harrying poor Covenanters to death on every hillside in Scotland. Nor would his lawyers let the king forget Charles I.'s attack on the Massachusetts charter, begun so early as 1635, or the grounds therefor, such as the unwarranted transfer of it to Boston, or the likelihood that but for the outbreak of the Civil War it would have been annulled by the Long Parliament itself. Obviously Massachusetts could not hope to be let alone by the home government which had just come in.

At first the king, graciously responding to the colony's humble petition, confirmed the charter granted by his father; but no sooner had he done so than the hot royalists about him began plotting to overthrow the same, and their purpose never slumbered till it was accomplished. Massachusetts was too prosperous and too visibly destined for great power in America to be suffered longer to go its independent way as hitherto.

The province—as yet, of course, exclud-

King Charles II.

ing Plymouth with its twelve towns and five thousand inhabitants—contained at this time, 1660, about twenty-five thousand souls, living in fifty-two towns. These were nearly all on the coast; Dedham,

Concord, Brookfield, Lancaster, Marlborough, and the Connecticut Valley hamlets of Springfield, Hadley, and Northampton being the most noteworthy exceptions. Though agriculture was the principal business, fishing was a staple industry, its product going to France, Spain, and the Straits. Pipe-staves, fir-boards, much material for ships, as masts, pitch and tar, also pork and beef, horses and corn, were shipped from this colony to Virginia, in return for tobacco and sugar either for home consumption or for export to England. Some iron was manufactured. The province enjoyed great prosperity. Boston stood forth as a lively and growing centre, and an English traveller about this time declared some of its merchants to be "damnable rich."

As their most precious possession the colonists prized their liberties, which they claimed in virtue of their original patent. In a paper which it put forth on June 10, 1661, the General Court asserted for the colony the right to elect and empower its own officers, both high and low, to make its laws, to execute the same without appeal so long as they were not repugnant to those of England, and to defend itself by force and arms when necessary, against every infringement of its rights, even from acts of Parliament or of the king, if prejudicial to the country or contrary to just colonial legislation. In a word Massachusetts, even so early, regarded itself to all intents and purposes an independent State, and would have proclaimed accordingly had it felt sufficiently strong.

Manifestly the king would not grant so much. On the occasion of his confirming the charter he demanded that the oath of allegiance be taken by the people of the colony; that justice be administered there in his name; and that the franchise be extended to all freemen of sufficient substance, with the liberty to use in worship, public and private, the forms of the English Church. The people obeyed but in part, for they would not even appear to admit the king's will to be their law. The franchise was slightly extended, in a grudging way, but no new religious privileges were at this time conceded. Unfortunately political and religious liberty were now in conflict. It was worse for the Baptists and Quakers that the king favored them, and the treatment which they received in the colony inclined them to the royalist side in the controversy.

In July, 1664, commissioners arrived in Boston with full authority to investigate the administration of the New England charters. Such a procedure not being provided for in the Massachusetts document, the General Court, backed by the citizens almost to a man, successfully prevented complainants from appearing before the commission. The commissioners having summoned the colony as defendant in a certain case, a herald trumpeted proclamation through the streets, on the morning set for the trial, inhibiting all from aiding their designs. The trial collapsed, and the gentlemen who had ordered it, baffled and disgusted, moved on to New Hampshire, there also to be balked by a decree of the Massachusetts Governor and Council forbidding the towns so much as to meet at their behest.

Vengeance for such defiance was delayed by Charles II.'s very vices. Clarendon's fall had left him surrounded by profligate aides, too timid and too indolent to face the resolute men of Massachusetts. They often discussed the contumacy of the colony, but went no further than words. Massachusetts was even encouraged, in 1668, forcibly to re-assert its authority in Maine, against rule either by the king or by Sir Ferdinando Gorges's heir as proprietary.

Its charter had assigned to the colony land to a point three miles north of the Merrimac. Bold in the favor of the Commonwealth, the authorities measured from the head-waters of that river. But Plymouth had originally claimed all the territory west of the Kennebec, and had sold it to Gorges. Charles II. favored the Gorges heirs against Massachusetts, and for some years previous to 1668 Massachusetts' power over Maine had been in abeyance. Ten years later, in 1678, to make assurance doubly sure, Massachusetts bought off the Gorges claimants, at the round price of twelve hundred and fifty pounds sterling.

From 1641 Massachusetts had borne sway in New Hampshire as well, ignoring John Mason's claim under Charles I.'s charters of 1629 and 1635, still urged by one of Mason's grandsons, backed by Charles II. Here Massachusetts was beaten. In July, 1679, New Hampshire was permanently separated from her, and erected into a royal province, of a nature to be explained in a subsequent chapter, being the earliest government of this kind in New England.

These territorial assumptions on the part of Massachusetts much increased the king's hostility. This probably would not have proved fatal had it not been re-enforced by the determination of the merchants and manufacturers of the mother-country to crush what they feared was becoming a rival power beyond seas. They insisted upon full enforcement of the Navigation Laws, which made America's foreign trade in a cruel degree subservient to English interest. So incorrigible was the colony, it was found that this end could be compassed only by the abrogation of the charter, so that English law might become immediately valid in Massachusetts, colonial laws to the contrary notwithstanding. Accordingly, in 1684, the charter was vacated and the colonists ceased to be free, their old government with its popular representation giving way to an arbitrary commission.

The other New England colonies—Plymouth, Rhode Island, Connecticut, and New Haven—had made haste to proclaim Charles II. so soon as restored to the throne, and to begin carrying on their governments in his name. That beautiful and able man, the younger Winthrop, sped to London on Connecticut's behalf, and, aided by his colony's friends at court, the Earls of Clarendon and Manchester and

Viscount Say and Seal, in 1662 secured to Connecticut, now made to include New Haven, a charter so liberal that it continued till October 5, 1818, the ground law of the State, then to be supplanted only by

John Winthrop the Younger.

a close vote. Under this paper, which declared all lands between the Narragansett River and the Pacific Ocean Connecticut territory, Connecticut received every whit of that right to govern itself which

Charles was so sternly challenging in the case of Massachusetts.

From this time on, as indeed earlier, Connecticut was for many years perhaps the most delightful example of popular government in all history. Connecticut and New Haven together had about ten thousand inhabitants. Their rulers were just, wise, and of a mind truly to serve the people. Here none were persecuted for their faith. Education was universal. Few were poor, none very rich. Nearly all supplies were of domestic production, nothing as yet being exported but a few cattle.

Under the second Charles Rhode Island fared quite as well as Connecticut. This was remarkable, inasmuch as the little colony of three thousand souls, in their four towns of Providence, Newport, Portsmouth, and Warwick, insisted on "holding forth the lively experiment"—and it proved lively indeed—"of full liberty in religious concernments." Charles did not oppose this, and Clarendon favored it, a motive of both here, as with Connecticut, being to rear in New England a power friendly to the Crown, that should rival and check Massachusetts. Both these commonwealths were granted absolute independence in all but name. No oath of allegiance to the king was demanded. Appeals to England were not provided for.

Though having no quarrel with the king, the two southern colonies were not without their trials. Connecticut, besides continual fear of the Dutch and the Indians, was much agitated by the controversy over the question whether children of moral parents not church members should be baptized, a question at length settled affirmatively by the so-called Half-Way Covenant. It also had its boundary disputes with Massachusetts, with Rhode Island—for Connecticut took the Narragansett River of its charter to be the bay of that name—and with New York, which, by the Duke of York's new patent, issued on the recovery of that province from the Dutch in 1674, reached the Connecticut River. During England's war with Holland, 1672-74, all the colonies stood in some fear of Dutch attacks.

Rhode Island had worse troubles than Connecticut. It, too, had boundary disputes, serious and perpetual; but graver by much were its internal feuds, caused partly by the mutual jealousy of its four towns, partly by the numerous and jarring religious persuasions here represented. Government was painfully feeble. Only with utmost difficulty could the necessary taxes be raised. Warwick in particular was for some time in arrears to John Clark, of Newport, for his invaluable services in securing the charter of 1663. Quakers and the divers sorts of Baptists valiantly warred each against other, using, with dreadful address, those most deadly of carnal weapons, tongue and pen. On George Fox's visit to the colony, Roger Williams, zealous for a debate, pursued the eminent Quaker from Providence to Newport, rowing thither in his canoe and arriving at midnight, only to find that his intended opponent had departed. The latter's champion was ready, however, and a discussion of four days ensued.

Before its sentence of death reached Massachusetts Charles II. was no more, and James II., his brother, had ascended

Sir Edmond Andros.

the throne. It was for a time uncertain what sort of authority the stricken colony would be called to accept. Already, as Duke of York, James II. had been Proprietary of Maine east of the Kennebec (Sagadahoc), as well as of Delaware, New Jersey, and New York. Now that he had the problem of ruling Massachusetts to solve, it naturally occurred to the king to make Sir Edmond Andros, already governor of New York, master also over the whole of English America from the Saint Croix to the Delaware.

In southern New England the reign of Andros wrought no downright persecution. He suspended the charters, and, with an irresponsible council in each colony, assumed all legislative as well as administrative power. Rhode Island submitted tamely. Her sister colony did the same, save that, at Hartford, according to good tradition, in the midst of the altercation about delivering the charter, prolonged into candle-light, suddenly it was dark, and the precious document disappeared to a secure place in the hollow trunk of an oak. This tree, henceforth called the Charter Oak, stood till prostrated by a gale on August 20, 1856.

But in Massachusetts the colonists' worst

fears were realized. Andros, with a council of his own creation, made laws, levied taxes, and controlled the militia. He had authority to suppress all printing-presses and to

The Charter Oak at Hartford.

encourage Episcopacy. In the latter interest he opened King's Chapel to the Prayer Book. His permission was required for any one to leave the colony. Extortionate fees and taxes were imposed. Puritans had to swear on the Bible, which they regarded wicked, or be disfranchised. Personal and proprietary rights were summarily set at naught, and all deeds to land were declared void till renewed—for money, of course. The citizens were reduced to a condition hardly short of slavery.

There is no describing the joy which pervaded New England as the news of the Revolution of 1688 flew from colony to colony. Andros slunk away from Boston, glad to escape alive. Drums beat and gala-day was kept. Old magistrates were reinstated. Town meetings were resumed. All believed that God had interposed, in answer to prayer, to bring deliverance to his people from popery and thraldom.

This revolution, ushering in the liberal monarchy of William and Mary, restored to Rhode Island and Connecticut their old charter governments in full. New Hampshire, after a momentary union with Massachusetts again, became once more a royal province. As to Massachusetts itself, a large party of the citizens now either did not wish the old state of things renewed, or were too timid to agree in demanding back their charter as of right. Had they been bold and united, they might have succeeded in this without any opposition from the Crown. Instead, a new charter was conferred, creating Massachusetts also a royal province, yet with government more liberal than the other provinces of this order enjoyed. The governor was appointed by the Crown, and could convene, adjourn, or dissolve the Legislature. With the consent of his council he also created the judges, from whose highest sentence appeal could be taken to the Privy Council. The governor could veto legislation, and the king annul any law under three years old.

If in these things the new polity was inferior to the old, in two respects it was superior: Suffrage was now practically universal, and every species of religious profession, save Catholicism, made legal. Also, Massachusetts territory was enlarged southward to take in all Plymouth, eastward to embrace Maine (Sagadahoc) and Nova

Scotia. Maine, henceforth including Sagadahoc, that is, all land eastward to the Saint Croix, remained part of Massachusetts till March 15, 1820, when it became a member of the Union by itself. Nova Scotia, over which Phips's conquest of Port Royal in 1690 had established a nominal rather than a real English authority, was assigned to France again by the Treaty of Ryswick, 1697.

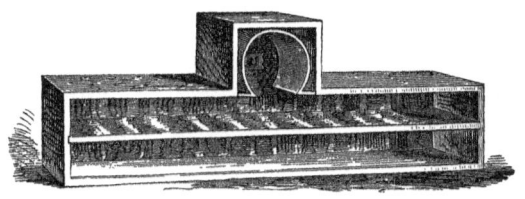

Box in which the Connecticut Charter was kept.

CHAPTER II.

KING PHILIP'S WAR

SIMULTANEOUSLY with the Stuart Restoration another cloud darkened the New England sky. Since the Pequot War, Indians and whites had in the main been friendly. This by itself is proof that our fathers were less unjust to the red men than is sometimes charged. They did assume the right to acquire lands here, and they had this right. The Indians were not in any proper sense owners of New England. They were few—by 1660 not more numerous than the pale-faces—and, far from settling or occupying the land, roamed from place to place. Had it been otherwise they, as barbarians, would have had no such claim upon the territory as to justify them in barring out civilization. However, the colonists did not plead this consideration. Whenever districts were desired to which Indians had any obvious title, it was both law and custom to pay them their price. In this Roger Williams and William Penn were not peculiar. If individual white men sometimes cheated in land trades, as in other negotiations, the aggrieved side could not, and did not, regard this as the white man's policy.

Yet little by little the Indians came to distrust and hate the rival race. It did not matter to the son of the forest, even if he thought so far, that the neighborhood of civilization greatly bettered his lot in many things, as, for instance, giving him market for corn and peltry, which he could exchange for fire-arms, blankets, and all sorts of valuable conveniences. The efforts to teach and elevate him he appreciated still less. As has been said, he loved better to disfurnish the outside of other people's heads than to furnish the inside of his own. What he felt, and keenly, was that the newcomers treated him as an inferior, were day by day narrowing his range, and slowly but surely reducing his condition to that of a subject people. Dull as he was, he saw that one of three fates confronted him: to perish, to migrate, or to lay aside his savage character and mode of life. Such thoughts frenzied him.

The beautiful fidelity of Massasoit to the people of Plymouth is already familiar. His son Alexander, who succeeded him, was of a spirit diametrically the reverse. Convinced that he was plotting with the Narragansets for hostile action, the Governor and Council of Plymouth sent Major Winslow to bring him to court—for it must be remembered that Massasoit's tribe, the Pokanokets, had through him covenanted, though probably with no clear idea of what this meant, to be subject to the Plymouth government. Alexander, for some reason, became fatally ill while at Plymouth under arrest, dying before reaching home. The Indians suspected poison.

His brother Philip now became sachem. Philip already had a grudge against the whites, and was rendered trebly bitter by the indignity and violence, if nothing worse, to which Alexander had been subjected. He resolved upon war, and in 1675 war was begun.

We shall never certainly know to what extent Philip was an organizer. We believe correct the view of Hubbard, the contemporary historian, that he had prepared a wide-spread and pretty well arranged conspiracy among the main tribes of New England Indians, which might have been fatal but for "the special providence of God," causing hostilities to break out ere the savages were ready. Palfrey challenges this view of the case, but on insufficient grounds.

One Sausaman, an educated Indian, previously Philip's secretary, had left him and joined the Christian Indians settled at Natick. There were by this time several such communities, and also, according to Cotton Mather, many able Indian preachers. At the risk of his life, as he insisted, Sausaman had warned the Plymouth magistrates that danger impended.

He was soon murdered, apparently by Philip's instigation. At least Philip never denied this, nor did he after this time ever again court friendly relations with Plymouth, which he had constantly done hitherto. On the contrary, re-enforcements of strange Indians, all ready for the war-path, were continually flocking to his camp, squaws and children at the same time going to the Narraganset country, manifestly for security.

The Plymouth authorities, preparing for war, yet sent a kind letter to the sachem advising him to peace. In vain. At Swanzey, the town nearest Mount Hope, Philip's home, Indians at once began to kill and ravage, and Majors Bradford and Cudworth marched thither with a force of Plymouth soldiers. A Massachusetts contingent re-enforced them there, and they prepared to advance. Seeing it impossible to hold his own against so many, Philip crossed to Pocasset, now Tiverton, and swept rapidly round to Dartmouth, Middleborough, and Taunton, burning and murdering as he went. He then retired again to Tiverton, but in a few days started with all his warriors for central Massachusetts.

Here the Nipmucks, already at war, which indicated an understanding between them and the Pokanokets, had attacked Mendon. The day after Philip joined them there was a fight at Brookfield, the Nipmucks and their allies being victorious. They proceeded to burn the town nearly entire, though the inhabitants who survived, after a three days' siege in a fortified house, were relieved by troops from Boston just in the nick of time.

The Connecticut Valley was next the theatre of war. Springfield, Hatfield, Deerfield, and Northfield were attacked, the last two having to be abandoned. At Hadley the onset occurred on a fast-day. The men rushed from their worship with their muskets, which were ready to hand in church, and hastily formed for battle. Bewildered by the unexpected assault, they were on the point of yielding, when, according to tradition, an aged hero with long beard and queer clothing appeared, placed himself at their head and directed their movements. His evident acquaintance with fighting restored order and courage. The savages were driven pell-mell out of town, but the pursuers looked in vain for their deliverer. If the account is correct, it was the regicide, General Goffe, who had been a secret guest in the house of the Rev. Mr. Russell. He could not in such danger refrain from engaging once again, as he had so often done during the Civil War in England, in the defence of God's people.

From Hadley a party went to Deerfield to bring in the wheat that had been left when the town was deserted. Ninety picked men, the "flower of Essex," led by Captain Lothrop, attended the wagons as convoy. On their return, about seven o'clock in the morning, by a little stream in the present village of South Deerfield, since called Bloody Brook in memory of the event, the soldiers dispersed somewhat in quest of grapes, then ripe, when a sudden and fatal volley from an ambush was delivered upon them. The men had left

The Monument at Bloody Brook.

their muskets in the wagons and could not regain them. Lothrop was shot dead, and but seven or eight of his company escaped alive. A monument marks the spot where this tragic affair occurred.

So early as July, 1675, Massachusetts and Connecticut, acting for the New England Confederation, had effected a treaty with the strong tribe of the Narragansets in southern Rhode Island, engaging them to remain neutral and to surrender any of Philip's men coming within their jurisdiction. This agreement they did not keep. After the attacks on Springfield and Hatfield in October, great numbers of the Pokanoket braves came to them, evidently welcomed. To prevent their becoming a centre of mischief, Connecticut, Massachusetts, and Plymouth despatched a thousand men to punish the Narragansets. They met the foe at the old Palisade, in the midst of a dense swamp in what is now South Kingstown, Rhode Island. The terrible cold which rendered this Narraganset campaign so severe had turned the marsh into a bridge, and at once on their arrival the soldiers, weary and hungry as they were from their long march, and spite of its being Sunday, advanced to the attack. Massachusetts was in front, then Plymouth, then Connecticut. Long and bitter was the fight. The Indians, perfect marksmen, took deadly aim at the leaders. Five captains were killed outright and as many

Goffe at Hadley.

more mortally wounded. The fort was taken, re-taken, and taken again, the whites at last, to make sure work, setting fire to the wigwams. The storming party lost in killed and wounded one-fifth of its number. This Swamp Fight, as it was called, broke forever the strength of the Narragansets, the tribe and its allies dispersing in all directions.

In 1676 central Massachusetts was again aflame. Lancaster was sacked and burned, its inhabitants nearly all either carried captive or put to death with indescribable atrocities. Mrs. Rowlandson, wife of the Lancaster minister, also her son and two daughters, were among the captives. We have this brave woman's story as subsequently detailed by herself. Her youngest, a little girl of six, wounded by a bullet, she bore in her arms wherever they marched, till the poor creature died of cold, starvation, and lack of care. The agonized mother begged the privilege of tugging along the corpse, but was refused. She with her son and living daughter were ransomed, after wandering up and down with the savages eleven weeks and five days.

From Mrs. Rowlandson's narrative we have many interesting facts touching the Indians' habits of life. They carried ample stores from Lancaster, but soon squandered them, and were reduced to a diet of garbage, horses' entrails, ears, and liver, with broth made of horses' feet and legs. The liver they seemed to prefer raw. Their chief food was ground-nuts. They also ate acorns, artichokes, beans, and various sorts of roots. They especially delighted in old bones, which, being heated to drive out maggots and worms, they first boiled for soup, then ground for use as meal.

The captive lady often saw Philip. At his request she made a shirt and a cap for his son, for which he paid her. Says Hubbard, "Such was the goodness of God to these poor captive women and children that they found so much favor in the sight of their enemies that they offered no wrong to any of their persons save what they could not help, being in many wants themselves. Neither did they offer any uncivil carriage to any of the females, nor ever attempt the chastity of any of them." So soon as negotiations were opened for Mrs. Rowlandson's release, Philip told her of this, and expressed the hope that they would succeed. When her ransom had arrived he met her with a smile, saying: "I have pleasant words for you this morning; would you like to hear them? You are to go home to-morrow." Twenty pounds were paid for her, raised by some ladies of Boston, aided by a Mr. Usher.

Hostilities now bore southeastward. Philip was in his glory. All the towns of Rhode Island and eastern Massachusetts were in terror, nearly all in actual danger. At Medfield twenty whites were killed. Deserted Mendon was burned. Weymouth was attacked, and eleven persons were massacred in the edge of Plymouth. In Groton and Marlborough every house was laid in ashes, as were all in lower Rhode Island up to Warwick, and in Warwick all but one. Sachem Canonchet of the Narragansets drew into ambush at Pawtuxet a band of Plymouth soldiers, of whom only one escaped. Canonchet was subsequently taken by Captain Denison and executed. Rehoboth lost forty houses, Providence nearly as many.

The Connecticut Valley was invaded afresh. Springfield, Hadley, Northampton, and Hatfield were once more startled by the war-whoop and the whiz of the tomahawk. Captain Turner, hearing of an Indian camp at the falls of the Connecticut, now called by his name, in Montague, advanced with a troop of one hundred and eighty horse, arriving in sight of the encampment at daylight. Dismounting and proceeding stealthily to within sure shot, they beat up the Indians' quarters with a ringing volley of musketry. Resistance was impossible. Those who did not fall by bullet or sword rushed to the river, many being carried over the falls. Three hundred savages perished, the English losing but one man. A large stock of the enemy's food and ammunition was also destroyed. Though so splendidly successful, the party did not return to Hadley without considerable loss, being set upon much of the way by Indians who had heard the firing at the falls and sped to the relief of their friends. Turner was killed in the meadows by Green River; his subordinate, Holyoke, then commanding the retreat.

Turner's victory brought the war to a crisis. The red men lacked resources. The whites had learned the secrets of savage warfare. They could no longer be led into ambush, while their foe at no time during the war ventured to engage them in open field. Large parties of Indians began to surrender; many roving bands were captured. Hostilities continued still many months in Maine, the whites more and more uniformly successful, till the Treaty of Casco, April 12, 1678, at last terminated the war.

Hunted by the English backward and forward, Philip was at last driven to his old home upon Mount Hope. Here Captain

Church, one of the most practised of Indian fighters, surprised him on the morning of August 12, 1676, encamped upon a little upland, which it is believed has been exactly identified near a swamp at the foot of the mountain. By residents in the neighborhood it is known as Little Guinea. At the first firing Philip, but partially dressed, seized gun and powder-horn and made for the swamp. Captain Church's ambush was directly in his front. An Englishman's piece missed fire, but an Indian sent a bullet through the Great Sachem's heart.

In this fearful war at least six hundred of the English inhabitants either fell in battle or were murdered by the enemy. A dozen or more towns were utterly destroyed, others greatly damaged. Some six hundred buildings, chiefly dwelling-houses, were consumed by fire, and over a hundred thousand pounds of colonial money expended, to say nothing of the immense losses in goods and cattle.

Not without propriety has the Pokanoket

chief been denominated a king. If not a
Charlemagne or a Louis XIV., he yet possessed
elements of true greatness. While
he lived his mind evidently guided, as his
will dominated and prolonged, the war.
This is saying much, for the Indian's disinclination
to all strenuous or continuous
exertion was pronounced and proverbial.
Philip's treatment of Mrs. Rowlandson
must be declared magnanimous, especially
as, of course, he was but a savage king,
who might reasonably request us not to
measure him by our rules. The other party
to the war we have a right to judge more
rigidly, and just sentence in their case must
be severe. Philip's sorrowing, innocent
wife and son were brought prisoners to
Plymouth, and their lot referred to the ministers.
After long deliberation and prayer
it was decided that they should be sold into
slavery, and this was their fate.

CHAPTER III.

THE SALEM WITCHCRAFT

THE home life of colonial New England was unique. Its like has appeared nowhere else in human history. Mostwise it was beautiful as well. In it religion was central and supreme. The General Court of Plymouth very early passed the following order: "Noe dwelling-howse shal be builte above halfe a myle from the meeting-howse in any newe plantacion without leave from the Court, except mylle-howses and fferme-howses." In laying out a village the meeting-house, as the hub to which everything was to be referred, was located first of all. The minister's lot commonly adjoined. Then a sufficiency of land was parcelled off to each freeholder whereon to erect his dwelling. Massachusetts from the first, and Plymouth beginning somewhat later, also made eminent provision for schools—all in the interest of religion.

The earliest residences were necessarily of logs, shaped and fitted more or less rudely according to the skill of the builder or the time and means at his disposal. There was usually one large room below, which served as kitchen, dining-room, sitting-room, and parlor, and on the same floor with this one or two lodging-rooms. An unfinished attic constituted the dormitory for the rising generation. A huge stone chimney, terminating below in a still more capacious fireplace, that would admit logs from four to eight feet in length, conveyed away the smoke, and with it much of the heat. This involved no loss, as wood was a drug. Communicating with the chimney was the great stone baking-oven, whence came the bouncing loaves of corn-bread, duly "brown," the rich-colored "pompion" pies, and the loin of venison, beef, or pork.

Over these bounties—and such they were heartily esteemed, however meagre—often as the family drew around the table, its head offered thanks to the heavenly Giver. Each morning, after they had eaten, he read a goodly portion of God's Word, never less than a chapter, and then, not kneeling but standing, led his household in reverent and believing prayer for protection, guidance, stimulus in good, and for every needed grace. What purity, what love of rectitude, what strength of will did not the builders of America carry forth from that family altar! He who would understand the richest side and the deepest moving forces of our national life and development must not overlook those New England fireside scenes.

Prayers ended, the "men folks" went forth to the day's toil. It was hard, partly from its then rough character, partly from poverty of appliances. For the hardest jobs neighbors would join hands, fighting nature as they had to fight the Indians, unitedly. Farming tools, if of iron or steel, as axe, mattock, spade, and the iron nose for the digger or the plough, the village blacksmith usually fashioned, as he did the bakepan, griddle, crane, and pothooks, for indoor use. Tables, chairs, cradles, bedsteads, and those straight-backed "settles" of which a few may yet be seen, were either home-made or gotten up by the village carpenter. Mattresses were at first of hay, straw, leaves, or rushes. Before 1700, however, feather beds were common, and houses and the entire state of a New England farmer's home had become somewhat more lordly than the above picture might indicate. The colonists made much use of berries, wild fruits, bread and milk, game, fish, and shellfish. The stock wandered in the forests and about the brooks, to be brought home at night by the boys, whom the sound of the cow-bell led. In autumn bushels upon bushels of nuts were laid by, to serve, along with dried berries and grapes, salted fish and venison, as food for the winter. Every phase and circumstance of this pioneer life reminded our fathers of their dependence upon nature and the

Supreme Power behind nature, while at the same time the continual need and application of neighbor's co-operation with neighbor brought out brotherly love in charming strength and beauty.

But to old New England religion, as a clerical, public, and organized affair, there is a far darker side. In the eighteenth century belief in witchcraft was nearly universal. In 1683 one Margaret Matron was tried in Pennsylvania on a charge of bewitching cows and geese, and placed under bonds of one hundred pounds for good behavior. In 1705 Grace Sherwood was ducked in Virginia for the same offence. Cases of the kind had occurred in New York. There was no colony where the belief in astrology, necromancy, second sight, ghosts, haunted houses and spots, love-spells, charms, and peculiar powers attaching to rings, herbs, etc., did not prevail. Such credulity was not peculiar to America, but cursed Europe as well. It seemed to flourish, if anything, after the Reformation more than before. Luther firmly believed in witchcraft. He professed to have met the Evil One in personal conflict, and to have vanquished him by the use of an inkstand as missile. Perhaps every land in Europe had laws making witchcraft a capital crime. One was enacted in England under Henry VIII., another in James I.'s first year, denouncing death against all persons "invoking any evil spirit, or consulting, covenanting with, entertaining, employing, feeding, or rewarding any evil spirit, or taking up dead bodies from their graves to be used in any witchcraft, sorcery, charm, or enchantment, or killing or otherwise hurting any person by such infernal arts." A similar statute was contained in the "Fundamentals" of Massachusetts, probably inspired by the command of Scripture, "Thou shalt not suffer a witch to live." This law, we shall see, was not a dead letter.

No wonder such a law was of more effect in New England than anywhere else on earth. The official religion of the Puritans was not only superstitious in general but gloomy in particular, and most gloomy in New England. Its central tenet, here at least, seemed to be that life ought to furnish no joy, men seeking to "merit heaven by making earth a hell." Sunday laws were severe, and rigidly enforced from six o'clock Saturday evening till the same hour the next. Not the least work was allowed unless absolutely necessary, nor any semblance of amusement. Boys bringing home the cows were cautioned to "let down the bars softly, as it was the Lord's day." Sunday travellers were arrested and fined. Men might be whipped for absence from church. A girl at Plymouth was threatened exile as a street-walker for smiling in meeting. Increase Mather traced the great Boston fire of 1711 to the sin of Sunday labor, such as carrying parcels and baking food. In Newport, some men having been drowned who, to say good-by to departing friends, had rowed out to a ship just weighing anchor, Rev. John Comer prayed that others might take warning and "do no more such great wickedness."

Sermons were often two hours long; public prayer half an hour. Worse still was what went by the name of music—doggerel hymns full of the most sulphurous theology, uttered congregationally as "lined off" by the leader—nasal, dissonant,

Increase Mather.

and discordant in the highest imaginable degree. The church itself was but a barn, homely-shaped, bare, and in winter cold as out-of-doors. At this season men wrapped their feet in bags, and women stuffed their muffs with hot stones. Sleepers were rudely awakened by the tithing-man's baton thwacking their heads; or, if females, by its fox-tail end brushing their cheeks. Fast-days were common. Prayer opened every public meeting, secular as well as religious. The doctrine of special providences was pressed to a ridiculous extreme. The devil was believed in no less firmly than God, and indefinitely great power ascribed to him. The Catechism—book second in authority only to the Bible—contained of his Satanic Majesty a cut, which children were left, not to say taught, to suppose as correct a likeness as that of Cromwell, which crowned the mantels of so many homes.

In a people thus trained the miracle is not that witchcraft and superstition did so much mischief, but so little. Had it not been for their sturdy Saxon good sense its results must have proved infinitely more sad. The first remarkable case of sorcery in New England occurred at Boston, in 1688. Four children of a pious family were affected in a peculiar manner, imitating the cries of cats and dogs, and complaining of pains all over their bodies. These were the regulation symptoms of witch-possession, which presumably they had often heard discussed. An old Irish serving-woman, indentured to the family, who already bore the name of a witch,

Cotton Mather.

was charged with having bewitched them, and executed, the four ministers of Boston having first held at the house a day of prayer and fasting.

Young Cotton Mather, grandson of the distinguished Rev. John Cotton, a man of vast erudition and fervent piety, was at this time colleague to his father, Increase

Mather, as pastor of the Boston North Church. His imagination had been abnormally developed by fasts and vigils, in which he believed himself to hold uncommonly close communication with the Almighty. His desire to provide new arms for faith against the growing unbelief of his time led him to take one of the "bewitched" children to his house, that he might note and describe the ways of the devil in her case. The results he soon after published in his "Memorable Providences Relating to Witchcrafts and Possessions." This work admitted no doubt as to the reality of the demoniac possessions, which indeed it affected to demonstrate forever. All the Boston ministers signed its preface, certifying to its "clear information" that "both a God and a devil, and witchcraft" existed. "Nothing too vile," it alleged, "can be said of, nothing too hard can be done to, such a horrible iniquity as witchcraft is." The publication excited great attention, and to it in no small measure the ensuing tragedy may be traced.

In February, 1692, three more subjects, children of Rev. Mr. Parris, minister at Danvers, then called Salem Village, exhibited bad witchcraft symptoms. The utmost excitement prevailed. Neighboring clergymen joined the village in fasting and prayer. A general fast for the colony was

Old Tituba the Indian

ordered. But the "devilism," as Cotton Mather named it, spread instead of abating, the children having any number of imitators so soon as they became objects of general notice and sympathy. Old Tituba, an Indian crone, who had served in Parris's family, was the first to be denounced as the cause. Two other aged females, one crazy, the other bed-ridden, were also presently accused, and after a little while several ladies of Parris's church. Whoso uttered a whisper of incredulity, general or as to the blameworthiness of any whom Parris called guilty, was instantly indicted with them.

On April 11th, the Deputy Governor held in the meeting-house in Salem Village a court for a preliminary examination of the prisoners. A scene at once ridiculous and tragic followed. When they were brought in, their alleged victims appeared overcome at their gaze, pretending to be bitten, pinched, scratched, choked, burned, or pricked by their invisible agency in revenge for refusing to subscribe to a covenant with the devil. Some were apparently stricken down by the glance of an eye from one of the culprits, others fainted, many writhed as in a fit. Tituba was beaten to make her confess. Others were

Lieutenant-Governor Stoughton.

tortured. Finally all the accused were thrown into irons. Numbers of accused persons, assured that it was their only chance for life, owned up to deeds of which they must have been entirely innocent. They had met the devil in the form of a small black man, had attended witch sacraments, where they renounced their Christian vows, and had ridden through the air on broomsticks. Such were the confessions of poor women who had never in their lives done any evil except possibly to tattle.

On June 2d, a special court was held in Salem for the definite trial. Stoughton, Lieutenant Governor, a man of small mind and bigoted temper, was president. The business began by the condemnation and hanging of a helpless woman. A jury of women had found on her person a wart, which was pronounced to be unquestionably a "devil's teat," and her neighbors remembered that many hens had died, animals become lame, and carts upset by her dreadful "devilism." By September 23d, twenty persons had gone to the gallows, eight more were under sentence, and fifty-five had "confessed" and turned informers as their only hope. The "afflicted" had increased to fifty. Jails were crammed with persons under accusation, and fresh charges of alliance with devils were brought forward every day.

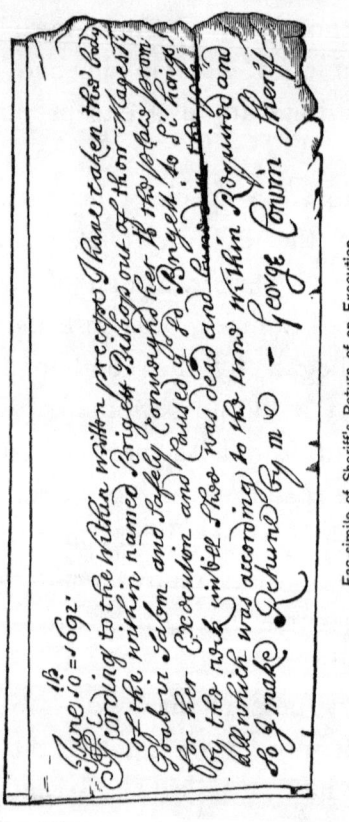

Fac-simile of Sheriff's Return of an Execution.

Some of the wretched victims displayed great fortitude. Goodman Procter lost his life by nobly and persistently—vainly as well, alas!—maintaining the innocence of his accused wife. George Burroughs, who had formerly preached in Salem Village, was indicted. His physical strength, which happened to be phenomenal, was adduced as lent him from the devil. Stoughton browbeat him through his whole trial. What sealed his condemnation, however, was his offer to the jury of a paper quoting an author who denied the possibility of witchcraft. His fervent prayers when on the scaffold, and especially his correct rendering of the Lord's Prayer, shook the minds of many. They argued that no witch could have gotten through those holy words correctly—a test upon which several had been condemned. Cotton Mather, present at the gallows, restored the crowd to faith by reminding them that the devil had the power to dress up like an angel of light. Rebecca Nurse, a woman of unimpeachable character hitherto, unable from partial deafness to understand, so as to explain, the allegations made against her, was convicted notwithstanding every proof in her favor.

Reaction now began. Public opinion commenced to waver. No one knew whose turn to be hanged would come next. Emboldened by their fatal success, accusers whispered of people in high places as leagued with the Evil One. An Andover minister narrowly escaped death. The Beverly minister, Hale, one of the most active in denouncing witches, was aghast when his own wife was accused. Two sons of Governor Bradstreet were obliged to flee for their lives, one for refusing, as a magistrate, to issue any more warrants, the other charged with bewitching a dog. Several hurried to New York to escape conviction. The property of such was seized by their towns. A reign of terror prevailed.

People slowly awoke to the terrible travesty of justice which was going on. Magistrates were seen to have overlooked the most flagrant instances of falsehood and contradiction on the part of both accusers and accused, using the baseless hypothesis that the devil had warped their senses. The disgusting partiality shown in the accusations was disrelished, as was the resort that had been had to torture. One poor old man of eighty they crushed to death because he would plead guilty to nothing. The authorities quite disregarded the fact that every one of the self-accusations had been made in order to escape punishment. These considerations effected a revolution in the minds of most people. Remonstrances were presented to the courts, securing reprieve for those under sentence of death at Salem. This so irritated the despicable Stoughton that he resigned.

The forwardness of the ministers therein turned many against the persecution. After the first victims had fallen at Salem, Governor Phips took their advice whether or not to proceed. Cotton Mather indited the reply. It thankfully acknowledges "the success which the merciful God has given to the sedulous and assiduous endeav·

ors of our honorable rulers to defeat the abominable witchcrafts which have been committed in the country, humbly praying that the discovery of those mysterious and mischievous wickednesses may be perfected." It is pleasant to note, after all, the ministers' advice to the civil rulers not to rely too much on "the devil's authority"—on the evidence, that is, of those possessed. The court heeded this injunction all too little, but by and by it had weight with the public, who judged that, as the trials appeared to be proceeding on devil's evidence alone, the farce ought to cease. The Superior Court met in Boston, April 25, 1693, and the grand jury declined to find any more bills against persons accused of sorcery. King William vetoed the Witchcraft Act, and by the middle of 1693 all the prisoners were discharged.

CHAPTER IV.

THE MIDDLE COLONIES

THE English conquest of New Netherland from the Dutch speedily followed the Stuarts' return to the throne. Cromwell had mooted an attack on Dutch America, and, as noticed in Chapter I., Connecticut's charter of 1662 extended that colony to include the Dutch lands. England based her claim to the territory on alleged priority of discovery, but the real motives were the value of the Hudson as an avenue for trade, and the desire to range her colonies along the Atlantic coast in one unbroken line. The victory was not bloody, nor was it offensive to the Dutch themselves, who in the matter of liberties could not lose. King Charles had granted the conquered tract to his brother, the Duke of York, subsequently James II., and it was in his honor christened with its present name of New York.

The Duke's government was not popular, especially as it ordered the Dutch land-patents to be renewed—for money, of course; and in 1673, war again existing between England and Holland, the Dutch recovered their old possession. They held it however for only fifteen months, since at the Peace of 1674 the two belligerent nations mutually restored all the posts which they had won.

The reader already has some idea of Sir Edmond Andros's rule in America. New York was the first to feel this, coming under the gentleman's governorship immediately on being the second time surrendered to England. Such had been the political disorder in the province, that Andros's headship, stern as it was, proved beneficial. He even, for a time, 1683–86, reluctantly permitted an elective legislature, though discontinuing it when the legislatures of New England were suppressed. This taste of freedom had its effect afterward.

When news of the Revolution of 1688 in England reached New York, Andros was in Boston. Nicholson, Lieutenant-Governor, being a Catholic and an absolutist, and the colony now in horror of all Catholics through fear of French invasion from Canada, Jacob Leisler, a German adventurer, partly anticipating, partly obeying the popular wish, assumed to function in Nicholson's stead. All the aristocracy, English or Dutch, and nearly all the English of the lower rank were against him. Leisler was passionate and needlessly bitter toward Catholics, yet he meant well. He viewed his office as only transitory, and stood ready to surrender it so soon as the new king's will could be learned; but when Sloughter arrived with commission as governor, Leisler's foes succeeded in compassing his execution for treason. This unjust and cruel deed began a long feud between the popular and the aristocratic party in the colony.

From this time till the American Revolution New York continued a province of the

Sloughter signing Leisler's Death Warrant.

Crown. Royal governor succeeded royal governor, some of them better, some worse. Of the entire line Bellomont was the most worthy official, Cornbury the least so. One of the problems which chiefly worried all of them was how to execute the navigation acts, which, evaded everywhere, were here unscrupulously defied. Another care of the governors, in which they succeeded but very imperfectly, was to establish the English Church in the colony. A third was the disfranchisement of Catholics. This they accomplished, the legislature concurring, and the disability continued during the entire colonial period.

Hottest struggle of all occurred over the question of the colony's right of self-taxation. The democracy stood for this with the utmost firmness, and even the higher classes favored rather than opposed. The governors, Cornbury and Lovelace, most frantically, but in vain, expostulated, scolded, threatened, till at last it became admitted by law in the colony that no tax whatever could, on any pretext, be levied save by act of the people's representatives.

Dutch America, it will be remembered, had reached southward to the Delaware River, and this lower portion passed with the rest to the Duke of York in 1664. The territory between the Hudson and the Delaware, under the name of New Jersey, he made over to Lord Berkeley and Sir George Carteret, proprietaries, who favored the freest institutions, civil and religious. The

Seal of the Carterets.

population was for long very sparse and, as it grew, very miscellaneous. Dutch, Swedes, English, Quakers, and Puritans from New England were represented.

After the English recovery Berkeley disposed of his undivided half of the province, subsequently set off as West Jersey, to one Bylling, a Quaker, who in a little time assigned it to Lawrie, Lucas, Penn, and other Quakers. West Jersey became as much a Quaker paradise as Pennsylvania. Penn with eleven of his brethren, also bought, of Carteret's heirs, East Jersey, but here Puritan rather than Quaker influence prevailed.

The Jersey plantations came of course under Andros, and after his fall its proprietors did not recover their political authority. For twelve years, while they were endeavoring to do this, partial anarchy cursed the province, and at length in 1702 they surrendered their rights to the Crown, the Jerseys, now made one, becoming directly subject to Queen Anne. The province had its own legislature and, till 1741, the same governors as New York. It

Seal of East Jersey.

also had mainly the same political vicissitudes, and with the same result.

William Penn, the famous Quaker, received the proprietorship of Pennsylvania in payment of a claim for sixteen thousand pounds against the English Government. This had been left him by his father, Sir William Penn, a distinguished naval com-

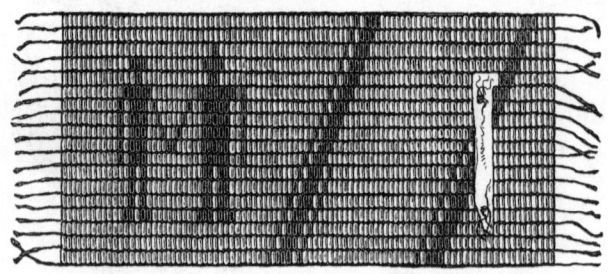

Wampum received by Penn in Commemoration of the Indian Treaty.

mander in the Dutch war of 1665–67, when he had borne chief part in the conquest of Jamaica.

William Penn was among the most cultivated men of his time, polished by study and travel, deeply read in law and philosophy. He had fortune, and many friends at court, including Charles II. himself. He needed

From the copy by Francis Race in the National Museum, Philadelphia.

but to conform, and great place was his. But conform he would not. True to the inner light, braving the scoffs of all his friends, expelled from Oxford University, beaten from his own father's door, imprisoned now nine months in London Tower, now six in Newgate, this heroic spirit persistently went the Quaker way. In despair of securing in England freedom for distressed consciences he turned his thoughts toward America, there to try his "holy experiment."

The charter from Charles II. was drawn by Penn's own hand and was nobly liberal. It ordained perfect religious toleration for all Christians, and forbade taxation save by the provincial assembly or the English Parliament. Under William and Mary, greatly to his grief, Penn was forced to sanction the penal laws against Catholics; but they were most leniently administered, which brought upon the large-minded proprietary much trouble with the home government.

As Pennsylvania, owing to the righteous

and loving procedure of Penn toward them, suffered nothing from the red men to the west, so was it fortunately beyond Andros's jurisdiction on the east. Once, from 1692, for two years, the land was snatched from Penn and placed under a royal commission.

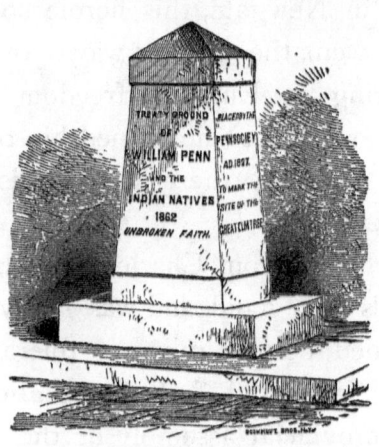

The Treaty Monument, Kensington.

Returning to England in 1684, after a two years' sojourn in America to get his colony started, the Quaker chief became intimate and a favorite with James II., devotedly supporting his Declaration of Indulgence toward Catholics as well as toward all Protestant dissenters. He tried hard but vainly to win William and Mary to the same policy. This attitude of his cost him dear, rendering him an object of suspicion to the men now in power in England. Twice was he accused of treasonable correspondence with the exiled James II., though never proved guilty. From 1699 to 1701 he was in America again, thereafter residing in England till his death in 1718. He had literally given all for his colony, his efforts on its behalf having been to him, so he wrote in 1710, a cause of grief, trouble, and poverty.

But the colony itself was amazingly prosperous. There were internal feuds, mainly petty, some serious. George Keith grievously divided the Quakers by his teachings against slavery, going to law, or service as magistrates on the part of Quakers, thus implying that only infidels or churchmen could be the colony's officials.

Fletcher's governorship in 1693–94, under the royal commission, evoked continual opposition, colonial privileges remaining intact in spite of him. The people from time to time subjected their ground-law to changes, only to render it a fitter instrument of freedom. In everything save the hereditary function of the proprietary, it was democratic. For many years even the governor's council was elective. The colony grew, im-

The Penn Mansion in Philadelphia.

migrants crowding in from nearly every European country, and wealth multiplied to correspond.

We have, dating from 1698, a history of Pennsylvania by one Gabriel Thomas, full of interesting information. Philadelphia was already a "noble and beautiful city," containing above 2,000 houses, most of them "stately," made of brick; three stores, and besides a town house, a market house, and several schools. Three fairs were held there yearly, and two weekly markets, which it required twenty fat bullocks, besides many sheep, calves, and hogs, to supply. The city had large trade to New York, New England, Virginia, West India, and Old England. Its exports were horses, pipe-staves, salt meats, bread-stuffs, poultry, and tobacco; its imports, fir, rum, sugar, molasses, silver, negroes, salt, linen, household goods, etc. Wages were three times as high as in England or Wales. All sorts of "very good paper" were made at Germantown, besides linen, druggets, crapes, camlets, serges, and other woollen cloths. All religious confessions were represented.

In 1712, such his poverty, the good proprietary was willing to sell to the Crown, but as he insisted upon maintenance of the colonists' full rights, no sale occurred. English bigots and revenue officials would gladly have annulled his charter, but his integrity had gotten him influence among English statesmen, which shielded the heritage he had left even when he was gone.

It is particularly to be noticed that till our Independence Delaware was most intimately related to Pennsylvania. Of Delaware the fee simple belonged not to Penn, but to the Duke of York, who had conquered it from the Dutch, as they from the Swedes. Penn therefore governed here, not as proprietary but as the Duke's tenant. In 1690–92, and from 1702, Delaware enjoyed a legislature by itself, though its governors were appointed by Penn or his heirs during the entire colonial period.

CHAPTER V.

MARYLAND, VIRGINIA, CAROLINA

THE establishment of Charles II. as king fully restored Lord Baltimore as proprietary in Maryland, and for a long time the colony enjoyed much peace and prosperity. In 1660 it boasted twelve thousand inhabitants, in 1665 sixteen thousand, in 1676 twenty thousand. Plantation life was universal, there being no town worthy the name till Baltimore, which, laid out in 1739, grew very slowly. Tobacco was the main production, too nearly the only one, the planters sometimes actually suffering for food, so that the raising of cereals needed to be enforced by law. For long the weed was also the money of the province, not disused for this even when paper currency was introduced, being found the less fluctuating in value of the two. Partly actual overproduction and partly the navigation acts, forcing all sales to be effected through England, fatally lowered the price, and Maryland with Virginia tried to establish a "trust" to regulate the output.

Charles, Second Lord Baltimore.

In its incessant and on one occasion bloody boundary disputes with Pennsylvania and Delaware, Maryland had to give in and suffer its northern and eastern boundaries to be shortened.

One of the most beautiful traits of early Maryland was its perfect toleration in religion. Practically neither Pennsylvania nor Rhode Island surpassed it in this. Much hostility to the Quakers existed, yet they had here exceptional privileges, and great numbers from Virginia and the North utilized these. All sorts of dissenters indeed flocked hither out of all European countries, including many Huguenots, and were made welcome to all the rights and blessings of the land.

But from the accession of Charles Calvert, the third Lord Baltimore, in 1675, the colony witnessed continual agitation in favor of establishing the English Church. False word reached the Privy Council that immorality was rife in the colony owing to a lack of religious instruction, and that Catholics were preferred in its offices. This movement succeeded, in spite of its intrinsic demerit, by passing itself off as part of the rising in favor of William and Mary in 1688–89.

James II. had shown no favor to Maryland. If its proprietary, as a Catholic, pleased him, its civil and religious liberty offended him more. He was hence not popular here, and the Marylanders would readily have proclaimed the new monarchs but for the accidental failure of the proprietary's commands to this effect to reach them. This gave occasion for one Coode, with a few abettors, to form, in April, 1689, an "Association in Arms for the Defence of the Protestant Religion, and for Asserting the Right of King William and Queen Mary to the Province of Maryland." The exaggerated representations of these conspirators prevailed in England. The proprietary, retaining his quit rents and export duty, was deprived of his political prerogatives. Maryland became a Crown province, Sir Lionel Copley being the first royal governor, and the Church of England received establishment therein.

The new ecclesiastical rule did not oppress Protestant dissenters, though very severe on Catholics, whom it was supposed necessary, here as all over America, to keep under, lest they should rise in favor of James II., or his son the Pretender.

The third Lord Baltimore died in 1714-15. The proprietaries after this being Protestants, were intrusted again with their old political headship. By this time a spirit of independence and self-assertion had grown up among the citizens, enforcing very liberal laws, and the vices of the sixth Lord, succeeding in 1751, made his subjects more than willing that he should, as he did, close the proprietary line.

Virginia, passionately loyal, at first gloried in the Restoration. This proved premature. It was found that the purely selfish Charles II. cared no more for Virginia than for Massachusetts. The Commonwealth's men were displaced from power. Sir William Berkeley again became governor, this time, however, by the authority of the assembly. A larger feeling of independence from England had sprung up in the colony in consequence of recent history at home and in the mother-land. It was developed still further by the events now to be detailed.

The Old Dominion contained at this time 40,000 people, 6,000 being white servants and 2,000 negro slaves, located mainly upon the lower waters of the Rappahannock, York, and James Rivers. Between 1650 and 1670, through large immigration from the old country, the population had increased from 15,000 to 40,000, some of the first families of the State in subsequent times arriving at this juncture. About eighty ships of commerce came each year from Great Britain, besides many from New England. Virginia herself built no ships and owned few; but she could muster eight thousand horse, had driven the Indians far into the interior, possessed the capacity for boundless wealth, and had begun to experience a decided sense of her own rights and importance. The last fact showed itself in Bacon's Rebellion, which broke out in 1676, just one hundred years before the Declaration of Independence. The causes of the insurrection were not far to seek.

The navigation acts were a sore grievance to Virginia as to the other colonies. Under Cromwell they had not been much enforced, and the Virginians had traded freely with all who came. Charles enforced them with all possible rigor, confining Virginia's trade to England and English ships manned by Englishmen. This gave England a grinding monopoly of tobacco, Virginia's sole export, making the planters commercially the slaves of the home government and of English traders. Duties on the weed were high, and mercilessly collected without regard to lowness of price. All supplies from abroad also had to be purchased in England, at prices set by English sellers. Even if from other parts of Europe, they must come through England, thus securing her a profit at Virginia's expense.

This was not the worst. The colonial government had always been abused for the ends of worthless office-holders from England. Now it was farmed out more offensively than ever. In 1673 Charles II.

donated Virginia to two of his favorites, Lords Arlington and Culpeper, to be its proprietaries like Penn in Pennsylvania and Baltimore in Maryland. They were to have all the quit rents and other revenues, the nomination of ministers for parishes, the right of appointing public officers, the right to own and sell all public or escheated lands : in a word, they now owned Virginia. This shabby treatment awoke the most intense rage in so proud a people. The king relented, revoked his donation, made out and was about to send a new charter. But it was too late: rebellion had already broken out.

The Indians having made some attacks on the upper plantations, one Nathaniel Bacon, a spirited young gentleman of twenty-eight, recently from England, applied to Sir William Berkeley for a commission against them. The governor declined to give it, fearing, in the present excited condition of the colony, to have a body of armed men abroad. Bacon, enraged, extorts the commission by force.

The result is civil war in the colony. The rebels are for a time completely victorious. Berkeley is driven to Accomac, on the eastern shore of the Chesapeake, but, suc-

Reverend Dr. Blair, First President of William and Mary College.

ceeding in capturing a fleet sent to oppose him, he returns with this and captures Jamestown. Beaten by Bacon in a pitched battle, he again retires to Accomac, and the colony comes fully under the power of his antagonist, the colonists agreeing even to fight England should it interpose on the governor's side, when a decisive change in affairs is brought about by the rebel leader's death.

The rebellion was now easily subdued, but it had soured and hardened old Governor Berkeley's spirit. Twenty-three in all were executed for participation in the movement. Charles II. remarked: "That old fool has hanged more men in that naked country than I for the murder of my father."

After Bacon's Rebellion the colonial annals show but a dull succession of royal governors, with few events specially interesting. Under the governorship of Lord Howard of Effingham, which began in 1684, great excitement prevailed in Virginia lest King James II. should subvert the English Church there and make Catholicism dominant, which indeed might possibly have occurred but for James's abdication in 1688.

Under Governor Nicholson, from 1690, the capital was removed from Jamestown to

Williamsburg, and the College of William and Mary founded, its charter dating from 1693. The Attorney-General, Seymour, opposed this project on the ground that the money was needed for "better pur-

George Monk, Duke of Albemarle.

poses" than educating clergymen. Rev. Dr. Blair, agent and advocate of the endowment, pleading: "The people have souls to be saved," Seymour retorted: "Damn your souls, make tobacco." But Blair persisted and succeeded, himself becoming first president of the college. The initial commencement exercises took place in 1700.

Governor Spotswood, who came in 1710, did much for Virginia. He built the first iron furnaces in America, introduced wine-culture, for which he imported skilled Germans, and greatly interested himself in the civilization of the Indians. He was the earliest to explore the Shenandoah Valley. It was also by his energy that the famous pirate "Blackbeard" was captured and executed. Lieutenant Maynard, sent with two ships to hunt him, attacked and boarded the pirate vessel in Pamlico Sound, 1718. A tough fight at close quarters ensued. Blackbeard was shot dead, his crew crying for quarter. Thirteen of the men were hung at Williamsburg. Blackbeard's skull, made into a drinking-cup, is preserved to this day. The great corsair's fate, Benjamin Franklin, then a printer's devil in Boston, celebrated in verse.

Carolina was settled partly from England, France, and the Barbadoes, and partly from New England; but mainly from Virginia, which colony furthermore furnished most of its political ideas.

In March, 1663, Carolina was constituted a territory, extending from 36° north latitude southward to the river San Matheo,

Lord Shaftesbury.

and assigned to a company of seven distinguished proprietaries, including General Monk, who had been created Duke of Albemarle, and John Locke's patron, the famous Lord Ashley Cooper, subsequently Earl of Shaftesbury. Governor Sir William

Berkeley, of Virginia, was also one of the proprietaries.

Locke drew up for the province a minute

Seal of the Proprietors of Carolina.

feudal constitution, but it was too cumbersome to work. Rule by the proprietaries proved radically bad. They were ignorant, callous to wrongs done by their governors, and indifferent to everything save their own profits. Many of the settlers too were turbulent and criminals, fugitives from the justice of other colonies. The difficulty was aggravated by Indian and Spanish wars, by negro slavery, so profitable for rice culture, especially in South Carolina, by strife between dissenters and churchmen, by the question of revenue, and by that of representation.

A proprietary party and a larger popular party were continually at feud, not seldom

John Locke.

with arms, support of the Church allying itself mainly with the former, dissent with the latter. Zealots for the Church wished to exclude dissenters from the assembly. Their opponents would keep Huguenot immigrants, whom the favor of the proprietaries rendered unwelcome, entirely from the franchise. The popular party passed laws for electing representatives in every county instead of at Charleston alone, and for revenue tariffs to pay the debt entailed by war. The proprietaries vetoed both. They even favored the pirates who harried the coast. Civil commotions were frequent and growth slow. Interference by the Crown was therefore most happy. From the time the Carolinas passed into royal hands, 1729, remarkable prosperity attended them both.

Assuming charge of Carolina, the Crown reserved to itself the Spanish frontier, and here, in 1732, it settled Oglethorpe, the able and unselfish founder of Georgia, under the auspices of an organization in form much like a mercantile company, but benevolent in aim, whose main purpose was to open a home for the thousands of Englishmen who were in prison for debt. Many Scotch and many Austrians also came. Full civil liberty was promised to all, religious liberty to all but papists. Po-

Savannah, from a Print of 1741.

litical strife was warm here, too, particularly respecting the admission of rum and slaves. Government by the corporators, though well-meaning, was ill-informed and a failure, and would have been ruinous to the colony but for Oglethorpe's genius and exertions. To the advantage of all, therefore, on the lapse of the charter in 1752, Georgia, like the Carolinas, assumed the status of a royal colony.

James Oglethorpe.

CHAPTER VI.

GOVERNMENTAL INSTITUTIONS IN THE COLONIES

THE political life, habits, and forms familiar to our fathers were such as their peculiar surroundings and experience had developed out of English originals. This process and its results form an interesting study.

The political unit at the South was the parish; in the North it was the town. Jury trial prevailed in all the colonies. Local self-government was vigorous everywhere, yet the most so in the North. The town regulated its affairs, such as the schools, police, roads, the public lands, the poor, and in Massachusetts and Connecticut also religion, at first by pure mass meetings where each citizen represented himself and which were both legislative and judicial in function, then by combining these meetings in various ways with the agency of selectmen. Where and so soon as a colony came to embrace several towns, representative machinery was set in motion and a colonial legislature formed, having two chambers nearly everywhere, like Parliament. The county, with the same character as at present, was instituted later than the oldest towns and parishes, but itself subsequently became, in thinly settled parts, the unit of governmental organization and political action, being divided into towns or parishes only gradually. Voting was subject to a property qualification, in some colonies to a religious one also; but no nobility of blood or title got foothold.

The relation of the colonial governments to England is a far more perplexing matter. From the preceding chapters it appears that we may distinguish the colonies, if we come down to about 1750, as either (1) self-governing or charter colonies, in which liberty was most complete and subjection to England little more than nominal; and

(2) non-self-governing, ruled, theoretically at any rate, in considerable measure from outside themselves. Rhode Island and Connecticut made up the former class. Of the latter there were two groups, the royal or provincial, including New Hampshire, Massachusetts, New York, New Jersey, Virginia, the Carolinas, and Georgia, and the proprietary, viz., Pennsylvania, Maryland, and Delaware.

Yet we are to bear in mind that many important constitutional and governmental changes had occurred by 1750. Massachusetts, as we have seen, had ceased to be self-governing as at first, yet it retained a charter which conferred large liberty. All the provincial colonies began as proprietary, and all the proprietary were for a time provincial.

Under Andros, New England stretched from the St. Croix to Delaware Bay. After 1689 the tendency in all parts of the country was strong toward civil freedom, which, favored by the changes and apathy of proprietaries and the ignorance and quarrels of the English ministry, gradually rendered the other colonies in effect about as well off in this respect as Rhode Island and Connecticut.

But unfortunately the legal limits and meaning of this freedom were never determined. Had they been, our Revolution need not have come. Monarchs continually attempted to stretch hither the royal prerogative, but how far this was legal was not then, and never can be, decided. The constitutional scope of a monarch's prerogative in England itself was one of the great questions of the seventeenth century, and remained serious and unsettled through the eighteenth. Applied to America the problem became angrier still, partly because giving a charter—and the colonies were all founded on such gift—was an act of prerogative.

English lawyers never doubted that acts of Parliament were valid in the colonies. The colonists opposed both the king's and the Parliament's pretensions, and held their own legislatures to be coördinate with the

Houses at Westminster. They claimed *as rights* the protection of *habeas corpus*, freedom from taxation without their consent, and all the Great Charter's guarantees. It was the habit of English theorizing on the subject to allow them these, if at all, as of grace. Repudiating the pretence that they were represented in Parliament, they likewise denied all wish to be so, but desired to have colonial legislatures recognized as concurrent with the English—each colony joined to the mother-country by a sort of personal union, or through some such tie as exists between England and her colonies to-day. Massachusetts theorists used as a valid analogy the relation of ancient Normandy to the French kings. Though no longer venturing to do so at home, monarchs freely vetoed legislation in all the colonies except Rhode Island and Connecticut. It was held that even these colonies were after all somehow subject to England's oversight.

On the subject of taxation there was continual dispute, misunderstanding, recrimination. The colonies did not object to providing for their own defence. They were willing to do this under English direction if asked, not commanded. Direct taxation for England's behoof was never once consented to by America, and till late never thought of by England. The English navigation laws, however, though amounting to taxation of America in aid of England, and continually evaded as unjust, were allowed by the colonies' legislative acts, and never seriously objected to in any formal way.

CHAPTER VII.

SOCIAL CULTURE IN COLONIAL TIMES

AMERICAN society rose out of mere untitled humanity; monarchy, guilds, priests, and all aristocracy of a feudal nature having been left behind in Europe. The year 1700 found in all the American colonies together some 300,000 people. They were distributed about as follows: New England had 115,000; New York, 30,000; New Jersey, 15,000; Pennsylvania and Delaware, 20,000; Maryland, 35,000; Virginia, 70,000; the Carolina country, 15,000. Perhaps 50,000 were negro slaves, of whom, say, 10,000 were held north of Mason and Dixon's line. What is now New York City had, in 1697, 4,302 inhabitants.

Passing on to 1754, we find the white population of New England increased to 425,000; that of the middle colonies, including Maryland, to 457,000; that of Virginia, the Carolinas, and Georgia, to 283,000. Massachusetts alone now had 207,000; Rhode Island, 35,000, Connecticut, 133,000; New York State (1756), 83,744. There were now not far from 263,000 negroes, of whom 14,000 lived in New England, 4,500 in Rhode Island. The total population of the thirteen colonies amounted to nearly a million and a half. At this time Philadelphia about equalled Boston in size, each having 25,000 inhabitants. At the Revolution Boston had grown to be the larger. New York, with from 15,000 to 18,000, constituted the centre of trade and of politics. The city and county of New York together numbered 13,046 inhabitants in 1756; 21,862 in 1771; 23,614 in 1786. The whole State, in 1771, had 146,144. Connecticut, in 1774, had 197,856. There are said to have been, so late as 1763, woods where the New York City Hall now stands.

From North to South the population decreased in density, but it increased in heterogeneity and non-English elements, and in illiteracy. The South had also the stronger aristocratic feeling. Slaves, as the above figures show, were far more numerous in that section. Their condition was also worse there.

A large proportion of the white population everywhere was of Saxon-Teutonic blood. The colonial leaders, and many others, at least in the North, were men who would have been eminent in England itself. Not a few New England theologians and lawyers were peers to the ablest of their time. Numbers of the common people read, reflected, debated. While profoundly religious, the colonists, being nearly all Protestants, were bold and progressive thinkers in every line, prizing discussion, preferring to settle questions by rational methods rather than through authority and tradition. We have observed that there are exceptions to this rule, like the treatment of Roger Williams, but they were exceptions. The colonists possessed in eminent degree energy, determination.

power of patient endurance and sacrifice. Their political genius, too, was striking in itself, and it becomes surprising if one compares Germany, in the unspeakable distrac-

Costume about the Middle of the Seventeenth Century.

tion of the Thirty Years' War, with America at the same period, 1618–1648, successfully solving by patience and debate the very problems which were Germany's despair.

In all the southern colonies the English Church was established, a majority of the people its members, its clergy supported by tithes and glebe. William and Mary secured it a sort of establishment also in New York and Maryland. Yet at no mo-

Costume about the Middle of the Seventeenth Century.

ment of the colonial period was there a bishop in America. No church building was consecrated with episcopal rites, no resident of America taken into orders without going to London.[1] Even in Vir-

[1] See, for these facts, *The Century* for May, 1888.

ginia, till a very late colonial period, the clergy retained many Puritan forms. Some would not read the Common Prayer. For more than a hundred years the surplice was apparently unknown there, sacraments administered without the proper ornaments and vessels, parts of the liturgy omitted, marriages, baptisms, churchings, and funerals solemnized in private houses. In some parishes, so late as 1724, the communion was partaken sitting. Excellent as were many of the clergymen, there were some who never preached, and not a few even bore an ill name. It was worst in Maryland, and "bad as a Maryland parson" became a proverb. The yearly salary in the best Virginia parishes was tobacco of about £100 value.

The Carolina clergy at first formed a superior class, as nearly all the early ministers were men carefully selected and sent out from England by the Society for the Propagation of the Gospel. Here there was special interest in the religious welfare of the slaves. All over the South the

Church ministers owed much to competition with those of sects, especially those of the Presbyterians, to which body belonged many of the Scotch and Irish immigrants after 1700. Dissent was dominant everywhere at the North. A vast majority of the people even in New York were dissenters, though the Episcopal clergy there successfully resisted all efforts against the Church tax, notwithstanding the fact that the same injustice in Massachusetts and Connecticut oppressed their brethren in those colonies. The New York clergy also fought every sort of liberal law, as to enable dissenting bodies of Christians to hold property. It was in good degree this attitude of theirs that filled the country, Virginia too, with such hatred of bishops.

But this spirit was fully matched by that of the Independent ministers in New England. Their dissent was aggressive, persecuting, puritanical. Meeting-houses were cold, sermons long and dry, music vocal only. Religious teaching and the laws it procured, foolishly assumed to regulate all the acts of life. Extravagance was denounced and fined. In 1750, the Massachusetts Assembly forbade theatres as "likely to encourage immorality and im-

Costume about the Middle of the Seventeenth Century.

piety." Rhode Island took similar action in 1762.

The ministers of Boston viewed bishops almost as emissaries of the devil. Herein in fact lay the primary, some have thought the deepest and most potent, cause of the

Revolution, since kings and the bishops of London incessantly sought to establish Anglicanism in Massachusetts, and English politicians deemed it outrageous that con-

Costume about the Middle of the Seventeenth Century.

formists should be denied any of that colony's privileges. For some time, under William and Mary's charter, in this province where Congregationalism had till now had everything its own way, only Church clergymen could celebrate marriage. In

New York and Maryland, too, hostility to the establishment greatly stimulated disloyalty. This was true even in Anglican Virginia, where the Church found it no easier to keep power than it was in Massachusetts to get power, and where the clergy were unpopular, concerned more for tithes than for souls.

Colleges were founded early in several colonies. Harvard dates from 1638; William and Mary, in Virginia, from 1693; Yale, from 1701; the College of New Jersey, from 1746, its old Nassau Hall, built in 1756 and named in honor of William III. of the House of Nassau, being then the largest structure in British America. The University of Pennsylvania dates from 1753; King's College, now Columbia, from 1754; Rhode Island College, now Brown University, from 1764. Educational facilities in general varied greatly with sections, being miserable in the southern colonies, fair in the central, excellent in the northern. In Virginia, during the period now under our survey, schools were almost unknown. In

Maryland, from 1728, a free school was established by law in each county. These were the only such schools in the South before 1770. Philadelphia and New York had good schools by 1700; rural Pennsylvania none of any sort till 1750, then only the poorest. A few New York and New Jersey towns of New England origin had free schools before the Revolution. Many Southern planters sent their sons to school in England. In popular education New England led not only the continent but the world, there being a school-house, often several, in each town. Every native adult in Massachusetts and Connecticut was able to read and write. In this matter Rhode Island was far behind its next neighbors.

Newspapers were distributed much as schools were. The first printing-press was set up at Cambridge in 1639. The first newspaper, *Publick Occurrences Foreign and Domestic*, was started in Boston in 1690. The first permanent newspaper, the *Boston News Letter*, began in 1704, and it had a Boston and a Philadelphia rival in 1719.

The *Maryland Gazette* was started at Annapolis in 1727, a weekly at Williamsburg, Va., in 1736. In 1740 there were eleven newspapers in all in the colonies: one each in New York, South Carolina, and Virginia

James Logan.

(from 1736), three in Pennsylvania, one of them German, and five in Boston. The *Connecticut Gazette* was started at New Haven in 1755; *The Summary*, at New London in 1758. The *Rhode Island Gazette* was begun by James Franklin, September

27, 1732, but was not permanent. The *Providence Gazette and Country Journal* put forth its first issue October 20, 1762. In 1775, Salem, Newburyport, and Portsmouth had each its newspaper. The first daily in the country, the *Pennsylvania Packet*, began in 1784.

Other literature of American origin flourished in New England nearly alone. It consisted of sermons, social and political tracts, poetry, history, and memoirs. The clergy were the chief but not the sole authors. Of readers, New York, Philadelphia, and Charleston had many. Much reading matter came from England. Charleston enjoyed a public library from 1700. About 1750 there were several others. That left to Philadelphia in 1751, by James Logan, comprised 4,000 volumes.

William and Mary had established a postal system for America, placing Thomas Neale, Esquire, at its head. The service hardly became a system till 1738. In ordinary weather a post-rider would receive the Philadelphia mail at the Susquehannah

River on Saturday evening, be at Annapolis on Monday, reach the Potomac Tuesday night, on Wednesday arrive at New Post, near Fredericksburg, and by Saturday evening at Williamsburg, whence, once a month, the mail went still farther south, to Eden-

King William.

ton, N. C. Thus a letter was just a week in transit between Philadelphia and the capital of Virginia. In New England, from here to New York, and between New York and Philadelphia, despatch was much better.

The learned professions also were best

patronized and had the ablest *personnel* in New England, where all three, but particularly the clergy, were strong and honored. Outside of New England, till 1750, lawyers and physicians, especially in the country parts, were poorly educated and little re-

Queen Mary.

spected. Each formidable disease had the people at its mercy. Diphtheria, then known as the throat disease, swept through the land once in about thirty years. Smallpox was another frequent scourge. In 1721 it attacked nearly six thousand persons in

Boston, about half the population, killing some nine hundred. The clergy, almost to a man, decried vaccination when first vented, proclaiming it an effort to thwart God's will. Clergymen, except perhaps in Carolina and Virginia, were somewhat better educated, yet those in New England led all others in this respect.

Colonial America boasted many great intellectual lights. President Edwards won European reputation as a thinker, and so did Franklin as a statesman and as a scientist. Linnæus named our Bartram, a Quaker farmer of Pennsylvania, the greatest natural botanist then living. Increase Mather read and wrote both Greek and Hebrew, and spoke Latin. He and his son Cotton were veritable wonders in literary attainment. The one was the author of ninety-two books, the other of three hundred and eighty-three. The younger Winthrop was a member of the Royal Society. Copley, Stuart, and West became distinguished painters.

Except for mails, there were in the colonies no public conveyances by land till just before the Revolution. After stage lines were introduced, to go from Philadelphia to Pittsburgh required seven days; from Philadelphia to New York, at first three, later two. The earliest coach to attain the last-named speed was advertised as "the flying machine." From Boston one would be four days travelling to New York, two to Portsmouth. Packet-boats between the main points on the coast were as regular and speedy as wind allowed. Stage-drivers, inn-keepers, and ship-captains were the honored and accredited purveyors of news.

Everywhere was great prosperity, little luxury. Paucity of money gave rise to that habit of barter and dicker in trade which was a mannerism of our fathers. Agriculture formed the basal industry, especially in the Southern colonies; yet in New England and Pennsylvania both manufactures and commerce thrived. Pennsylvania's yearly foreign commerce exceeded 1,000,000 pounds sterling, requiring 500 vessels and more than 7,000 seamen. From Pennsylvania, in 1750, 3,000 tons of pig-iron were exported. The annual production of iron in Maryland just before the Revolution reached 25,000 tons of pig, 500 of bar. The business of marine insurance began in this country at Philadelphia in 1721, fire insurance at Boston in 1724. New England produced timber, ships, rum, paper, hats, leather, and linen and woollen cloths, the first three for export.

In country places houses were poor save on the great estates, south, but in the cities there were many fine mansions before 1700. From this year stoves began to be used. Glass windows and paper hangings were first seen not far from 1750.

The colonists ate much flesh, and nearly all used tobacco and liquor freely. Finest ladies snuffed, sometimes smoked. Little coffee was drunk, and no tea till about 1700. Urban life was social and gay. In the country the games of fox and geese, three and twelve men morris, husking bees and quilting bees were the chief sports.

Tableware was mostly of wood, though many had pewter, and the rich much silver. The people's ordinary dress was of homemade cloth, but not a few country people still wore deerskin. The clothing of the rich was imported, and often gaudy with tasteless ornament. Wigs were common in the eighteenth century, and all head-dress stupidly elaborate.

William Lang, of Boston, advertises in 1767 to provide all who wish with wigs "in the most genteel and polite taste," assuring judges, divines, lawyers, and physicians, "because of the importance of their heads, that he can assort his wigs to suit their respective occupations and inclinations." He tells the ladies that he can furnish any one of them with "a nice, easy, genteel, and polite construction of rolls, such as may tend to raise their heads to any pitch they desire."

"Everybody wore wigs in 1750, except convicts and slaves. Boys wore them, servants wore them, Quakers wore them, paupers wore them. The making of wigs was an important branch of industry in Great Britain. Wigs were of many styles and prices. Some dangled with curls; and they were designated by a great variety of names, such as tyes, bobs, majors, spencers, foxtails, twists, tetes, scratches, full-bottomed dress bobs, cues, and perukes. The people of Philadelphia dressed as the actors of our theatres now dress in old English comedy. They walked the streets in bright-colored and highly decorated coats, three-cornered hats, ruffled shirts and wristbands, knee-breeches, silk stockings, low shoes, and silver buckles."[1] Lord Stirling, one of Washington's generals, had a clothing inventory like a king: a "pompidou" cloth coat and vest, breeches with gold lace, a crimson and figured velvet coat, seven scarlet vests, *et cetera, et cetera.*

The wigs encountered the zealous hostility of many, among these Judge Samuel Sewall. His highest eulogy on a departed worthy was: "The welfare of the poor was much upon his spirit, and he abominated

---

[1] Mrs. M. J. Lamb, in *Magazine of Am. History*, August. 1888.

periwigs." A member of the church at Newbury, Mass., refused to attend communion because the pastor wore a wig, believing that all who were guilty of this

Chief Justice Sewall.

practice would be damned if they did not repent. A meeting of Massachusetts Quakers solemnly expressed the conviction that the wearing of extravagant and superfluous wigs was wholly contrary to the truth.

There was an aristocracy, of its kind, in all the colonies, but it was far the strongest in the South. Social lines were sharply drawn, an "Esquire" not liking to be accosted as "Mr.," and each looking down somewhat upon a simple "Goodman." These gradations stood forth in college catalogues and in the location of pews in churches. The Yale triennial catalogue until 1767 and the Harvard triennial till 1772 arrange students' names not alphabetically or according to attainments, but so as to indicate the social rank of their families. Memoranda of President Clap, of Yale, against the names of youth when admitted to college, such as "Justice of the Peace," "Deacon," "of middling estate much impoverished," reveal how hard it sometimes was properly to grade students socially. At the South, regular mechanics, like all free laborers, were few and despised. The indentured servants, very numerous in several colonies, differed little from slaves. David Jamieson, attorney-general of New York in 1710, had been banished from Scotland as a Covenanter and sold in New Jersey as a four years' redemptioner to pay transportation expenses. Such servants were continually running away, which may have aided in abolishing the system. Paupers

The Pillory.

and criminals were fewest in New England. All the colonies imprisoned insolvent criminals, though dirt and damp made each prison a hell. All felonies were awarded capital punishment, and many minor crimes incurred barbarous penalties. Whipping-post, pillory, and stocks were in frequent use. So late as 1760 women were publicly whipped. At Hartford, in 1761, David Campbell and Alexander Pettigrew, for the burglary of two watches, received each fifteen stripes, the loss of the right ear, and the brand-mark "B" on the forehead. Pettigrew came near losing his life from the profuse bleeding which ensued. A husband killing his wife was hanged. A wife killing her husband was burned, as were slaves who slew their masters.

In care for the unfortunate and in the study and in all applications of social science, Philadelphia led. The Pennsylvania Hospital, the first institution of the kind in America, was founded in 1751. The Philadelphia streets were the first to be lighted; those of New York next; those of Boston not till 1773. Before the end of the period now before us Philadelphia and New York also had night patrols.

Signature of Jolliet (old spelling).

CHAPTER VIII.

ENGLAND AND FRANCE IN AMERICA

WORKING upward from the mouth of the St. Lawrence to the source of this and of the Mississippi, and then down the latter river, Franciscans and Jesuits their pioneers,

Totem of the Sioux.

braving dreadful hardships and dangers in efforts, more courageous than successful, to convert the Indians, the French had come to control that great continental highway and boldly to claim for France the entire heart of North America.

In 1659, Groseilliers and Radisson penetrated beyond Lake Superior, and dwelt for a time among the Sioux, who knew of the Mississippi River. Next year Groseil-

A Sioux Chief.

liers went thither again, accompanied by the Jesuit Menard and his servant, Guérin. In 1661 Menard and Guérin pushed into what is now Wisconsin, and may have seen the Mississippi. These explorations made the French familiar with the copper mines of Lake Superior, and awakened the utmost zeal to see the Great River of which the Indians spoke. La Salle probably discovered the Ohio in 1670, and traced it down to the falls at Louisville. His main eulogist holds that he even reached the Mississippi at that time, some three years

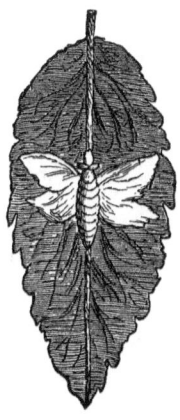

Totem of the Illinois.

earlier than Joliet, but this is not substantiated. We also reject the belief that he reached the stream by way of the Chicago portage in 1671.

In 1672 Count Frontenac, Governor of New France, despatched Louis Joliet to discover the Great River. He reached the

Strait of Mackinaw in December, and there Père Marquette joined him. In May, next year, they paddled their canoes up the Fox River and tugged them across the portage into the Wisconsin, which they descended, entering the Father of Waters June 17, 1673. They floated down to the mouth of the Arkansas and then returned, their journey back being up the Illinois and Desplaines Rivers. Joliet gave his name to the peak on the latter stream which the city of Joliet, Ill., near by, still retains. Joliet arrived at Quebec in August, 1674, having in four months journeyed over twenty-five hundred miles.

It thus became known how close the upper waters of the great rivers, St. Lawrence and Mississippi, were to each other, and that the latter emptied into the Gulf of Mexico instead of the South Sea (Pacific); yet, as the Rocky Mountains had not then been discovered, it was for long believed that some of the western tributaries of the Great River led to that western ocean.

In 1676 Raudin, and three years later,

The Reception of Joliet and Marquette by the Illinois.

Du Lhut, visited the Ojibwas and Sioux west of Lake Superior. Du Lhut reached the upper waters of the Mississippi at Sandy Lake. He went there again in 1680. In 1682 La Salle crossed the Chicago portage and explored the lower Mississippi all the way to the Gulf, taking possession of the entire valley in the name of France and naming it Louisiana. Nicholas Perrot travelled by way of the Fox and Wisconsin Rivers to the upper Mississippi in 1685, and again in 1688. It is in his writings that the word "Chicago" first appears in literature.

There were thus between the two great valleys, 1, the Superior route; 2, the Wisconsin and Fox route; 3, the Illinois River route, whether by the Kankakee, La Salle's way, or by the south branch of the Chicago River, Joliet's way; and 4, the route by the Wabash and Ohio. The Wabash, too, could be approached either from Lake Erie or from Lake Michigan, through St. Joseph's River. At high water, canoes often passed from Lake Michigan into the Mississippi without portage.

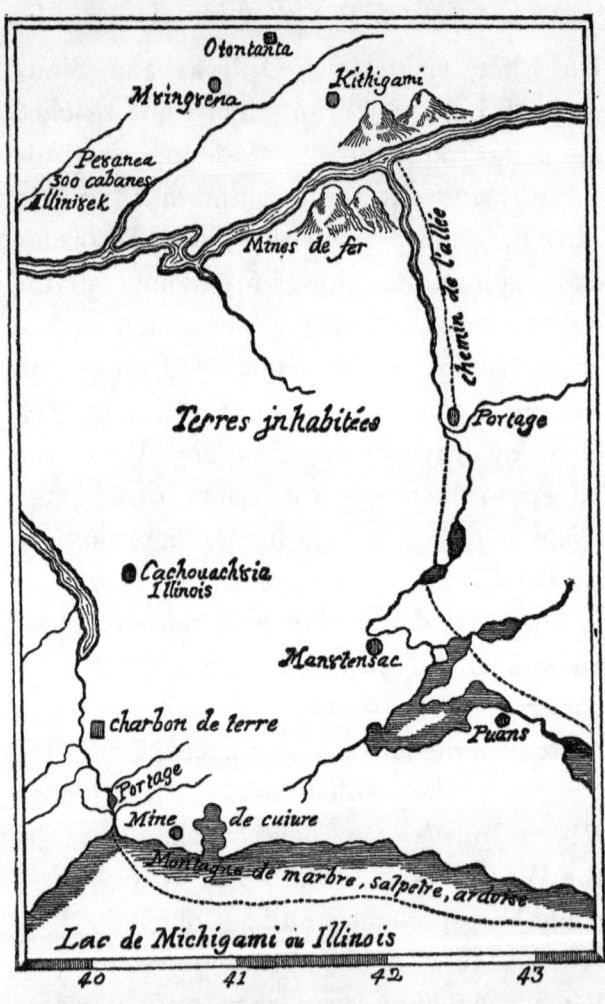

A Part of the Map Published in Paris by Thevenot as "Marquette's Map." It shows the route taken by Joliet across Wisconsin from the Baie des Puans (now Green Bay) to the Mississippi River, also part of the return journey, that is, from the present site of Chicago, northward along Lake Michigan.

La Salle had the ambition to get to the South Sea from the Mississippi. Governor De la Barre, who followed Frontenac, opposing him, he repaired to France, where he succeeded in winning Louis XIV. to his

Louis XIV.

plan. At the head of a well-equipped fleet he sailed for the mouth of the Mississippi, reaching land near Matagorda Bay on the first day of the year 1685. Not finding the Mississippi, La Salle's officers mutinied.

The expedition broke up into parties, wandering here and there, distressed by Indian attacks and by treachery among themselves La Salle was shot by his own men. Nearly all his followers perished, but a small party at last discovered the river and ascended it to Fort St. Louis on the Illinois, reaching France *via* Quebec. In this expedition

Coins Struck in France for the Colonies.

France took possession of Texas, nor did she ever relinquish the claim till, in 1763, the whole of Louisiana west of the Mississippi was ceded to Spain. La Salle's ill-starred attempt led later to the planting of French colonies by D'Iberville at Biloxi Island, in Mobile Bay, soon abandoned, and at Poverty Point, on the Mississippi; and still later to the settlement of New Orleans and vicinity. Growth in these parts was

Assassination of La Salle.

slow, however. So late as 1713 there were not over three hundred whites in the entire Mississippi Valley.

By this time French traders had set foot on every shore of the great lakes and explored nearly every stream tributary thereto. The English, pushing westward more and

New Orleans in 1719.

more, were trying to divide with them the lucrative business of fur-trading, and each nation sought to win to itself all the Indians it could. The Mohawks and their confederates of the Five Nations, now equipped and acquainted with fire-arms, spite of alternate overtures and threats from the French, remained firm friends to the English, who more and more invaded those vast and fertile western ranges. It grew to be the great question of the age this side the Atlantic, whether England or France should control the continent. King William's war, declared in 1689, was therefore certain to rage in America as well as in Europe.

One sees by a glance at the map what advantage France had in this struggle. It possessed the best fishing grounds and fur-producing districts, and fish and furs were at first the only exports of value from the north of America. The French, too, held

Signature of D'Iberville.

all the water-ways to the heart of the continent. Coming up Lake Champlain they could threaten New York and New England from the rear. The colonies farther south they shut in almost as straitly, French bullets whistling about any Englishman's ears the instant he appeared beyond the mountains.

In other respects England had the advantage. In population English America had become as superior as French America was territorially, having 1,116,000 white inhabitants in 1750, to about 80,000 French. The English colonies were also more convenient to the mother-country, and the better situated for commerce both coastwise and across the ocean. Among the English, temper for mere speculation and adventure decayed very early, giving way to the conviction that successful planting depended wholly upon persistent, energetic toil.

A piece of fortune more important yet was their relatively free religious and political system. Toleration in religion was large. Self-government was nearly complete internally, and indeed externally, till the navigation acts. Canada, on the other hand, was oppressed by a feudal constitution in the state, settlers being denied the fee simple of their lands, and by Jesuits in Church. "New France could not grow," says Parkman, "with a priest on guard at the gate to let in none but such as pleased him. In making Canada a citadel of the

The Attack on Schenectady.

state religion, the clerical monitors of the Crown robbed their country of a transatlantic empire." Thus the Huguenots, France's best emigrants to America, did not come to New France, but to New England and the other Protestant colonies.

The Indian hostilities which heralded King William's War began August 13, 1688. Frontenac prepared to capture Albany and even Manhattan. He did not accomplish so much; but on the night of February 8, 1689-90, his force of ninety Iroquois and over a hundred Frenchmen fell upon Schenectady, killed sixty, and captured eighty or ninety more. Only a corporal's guard escaped to Albany with the sad news. This attack had weighty influence, as occasioning the first American congress. Seven delegates from various colonies assembled at New York on May 1, 1690, to devise defence against the northern invaders.

The eastern Indians were hardly at rest from Philip's War when roused by the French to engage in this. An attack was made upon Haverhill, Mass., and Hannah Dustin, with a child only a few days old, another woman, and a boy, was led captive to an Indian camp up the Merrimac.

The savages killed the infant, but thereby steeled the mother's heart for revenge. One night the three prisoners slew their sleeping guards and, seizing a canoe, floated

Hannah Dustin's Escape

down to their home. Dover was attacked June 27, 1689, twenty-three persons killed, and twenty-nine sold to the French in Canada. Indescribable horrors occurred at Oyster River, at Salmon Falls, at Casco, at Exeter, and elsewhere.

In 1702 Queen Anne's War began, and in this again New England was the chief sufferer. The barbarities which marked it were worse than those of Philip's War. De Rouville, with a party of French and savages, proceeded from Canada to Deerfield, Mass. Fearing an attack, the villagers meant to be vigilant, but early on a February morning, 1704, the wily enemy, skulking till the sentinels retired at daylight, managed to effect a surprise. Fifty were killed and one hundred hurried off to Canada. Among these were the minister, Mr. Williams, and his family. Twenty years later a white woman in Indian dress entered Deerfield. It was one of the Williams daughters. She had married an Indian in Canada, and now refused to desert him. Cases like this, of which there were many in the course of these frightful wars, seemed to the settlers harder to bear than death. Massachusetts came so to dread the atrocious foe, that fifteen pounds were offered by public authority for an Indian man's scalp, eight for a child's or a woman's.

Governor Spotswood urged aggression on the French to the west; Governor

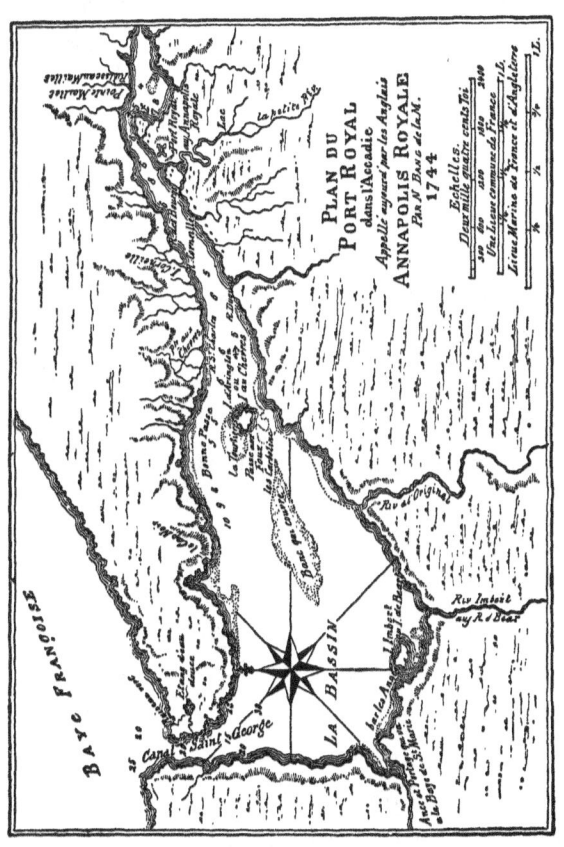

Plan of Port Royal, Nova Scotia.

Hunter of New York had equal zeal for a movement northward. New York raised

600 men and the same number of Iroquois, voting 10,000 pounds of paper money for their sustenance. Connecticut and New Jersey sent 1,600 men. A force of 4,000 in all mustered at Albany under Nicholson of New York. They were to co-operate against Montreal with the naval expedition of 1711, commanded by Sir Hoveden Walker. Walker failed ignominiously, and Nicholson, hearing of this betimes, saved himself by retreating.

Sir William Phips had captured Port Royal in 1690, and Acadia was annexed to Massachusetts in 1692. In 1691 the French again took formal possession of Port Royal and the neighboring country. In 1692 an ineffectual attempt was made to recover it, but by the Treaty of Ryswick, 1697, it was explicitly given back to France.

At the inception of Queen Anne's War, in 1702, there were several expeditions from New England to Nova Scotia; in 1704 and 1707 without result. That of 1710 was more successful. It consisted of four regiments and thirty-six vessels, besides troop and store ships and some marines. Port Royal capitulated, and its name was changed to Annapolis, in honor of Queen Anne. Acadia never again came under

Queen Anne.

French control, and was regularly ceded to England by the Treaty of Utrecht, 1713. Notwithstanding this, however, French America still remained substantially intact.

If the great struggle for the Ohio Valley

now became a silent one, it was none the less earnest. Spotswood had opened a road across the Blue Ridge in 1716. In 1721 New Yorkers began settling on Oswego River, and they finished a fort there by 1726. Closer alliance was formed with the Five Nations. The French governor of Quebec in 1725 pleaded that Niagara must be fortified, and on his successor was urged the necessity of reducing the Oswego garrison. It was partly to flank Oswego that the French pushed up Lake Champlain to Crown Point and built Fort St. Frederick.

The Treaty of Utrecht had left Cape Breton Island to France. The French at once strongly fortified Louisburg and invited thither the French inhabitants of Acadia and Newfoundland, which had also been ceded to Great Britain. Many went, though the British governors did much to hinder removal. This irritated the French authorities, and the Indian atrocities of 1723-24 at Dover and in Maine are known to have been stimulated from Montreal.

Father Rasle, an astute and benevolent French Jesuit who had settled among the Indians at Norridgewock, became an agent of this hostile influence. In an English

Governor Shirley.

attack, August 12, 1724, Rasle's settlement was broken up and himself killed. The Indians next year made a treaty, and peace prevailed till King George's War.

This opened in 1744, England against France once more, and in 1745 came the capture of Louisburg, then the Gibraltar of America. This was brought about through the energy of Governor Shirley, of Massachusetts, the most efficient English com-

Sir William Pepperrell.

mander this side the Atlantic. That commonwealth voted to send 3,250 men, Connecticut 500, New Hampshire and Rhode Island each 300. Sir William Pepperrell, of Kittery, Me., commanded, Richard Gridley, of Bunker Hill fame, being his chief of artillery. The expedition consisted of thirteen armed vessels, commanded by Captain Edward Tyng, with over 200 guns, and about ninety transports. The Massachusetts troops sailed from Nantasket March 24th, and reached Canso, April 4th. "Rhode Island," says Hutchinson, "waited until a better judgment could be made of the event, their three hundred not arriving until after the place had surrendered." The expedition was very costly to the colonies participating, and four years later England reimbursed them in the sum of £200,000. Yet at the disgraceful peace of Aix-la-Chapelle, in 1748, she surrendered Louisburg and all Cape Breton to France again.

In 1746 French and Indians from Crown Point destroyed the fort and twenty houses at Saratoga, killing thirty persons, and capturing sixty. Orders came this year from England to advance on Crown Point and Montreal, upon Shirley's plan, all the colonies as far south as Virginia being commanded to aid. Quite an army mustered at Albany. Sir William Johnson succeeded in rousing the Iroquois, whom the French had been courting with unprecedented assiduity. But D'Anville's fleet threatened. The colonies wanted their troops at home. Inactivity discouraged the soldiers, alienated the Indians. At last news came that the Canada project was abandoned, and in 1748 the Peace of Aix-la-Chapelle was declared.

This very year France began new efforts to fill the Ohio Valley with emigrants. Virginia did the same. To anticipate the English, the French sent Bienville to bury engraved leaden plates at the mouths of streams. They also fortified the present sites of Ogdensburg and Toronto. Even now, therefore, France's power this side the Atlantic was not visibly shaken. The continental problem remained unsolved.

CHAPTER IX.

THE FRENCH AND INDIAN WAR

THE Peace of Aix-la-Chapelle had been made only because the contestants were tired of fighting. In America, at least, each at once began taking breath and preparing to renew the struggle. Not a year passed that did not witness border quarrels more or less bloody. The French authorities filled the Ohio and Mississippi valleys with military posts; English settlers pressed persistently into the same to find homes. In this movement Virginia led, having in 1748 formed, especially to aid western settlement, the Ohio Company, which received from the king a grant of five hundred thousand acres beyond the Alleghanies. A road was laid out between the upper Potomac and the present Pittsburgh, settlements were begun along it, and efforts made to conciliate the savages.

One of the frontier villages was at what

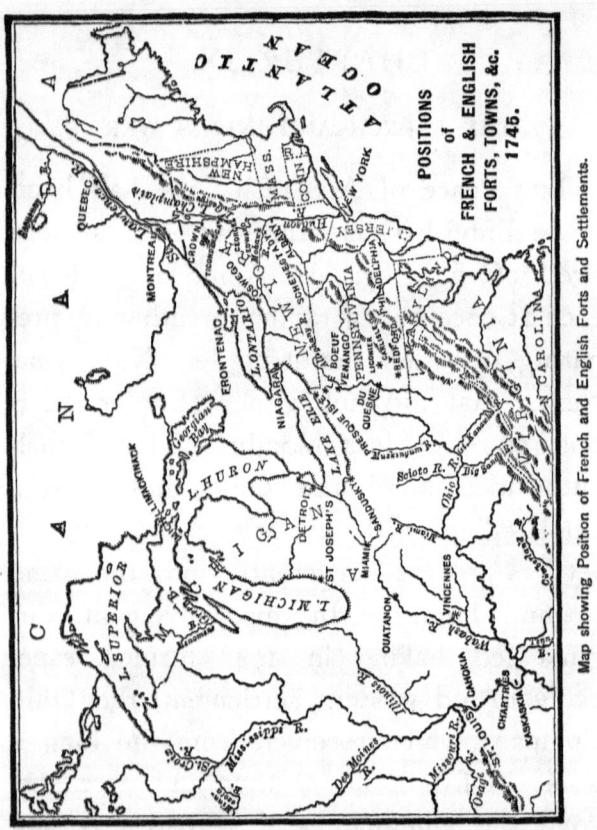

Map showing Position of French and English Forts and Settlements.

is now Franklin, Penn., and the location involved Virginia with the colony of Penn-

The Ambuscade.

sylvania. As commissioner to settle the dispute George Washington was sent out.

The future Father of his Country was of humble origin. Born in Westmoreland County, Va., "about ten in ye morning of ye 11th day of February, 1731-32," as recorded in his mother's Bible, he had been an orphan from his earliest youth. His education was of the slenderest. At sixteen he became a land surveyor, leading a life of the roughest sort, beasts, savages, and hardy frontiersmen his constant companions, sleeping under the sky and cooking his own coarse food. No better man could have been chosen to thread now the Alleghany trail.

Washington reported the French strongly posted in western Pennsylvania on lands claimed by the Ohio Company. Virginia fitted out an expedition to dislodge them. Of this Washington commanded the advance. Meeting at Great Meadows the French under Contrecœur, commander of Fort Du Quesne (Pittsburgh), he was at first victorious, but the French were re-enforced before he was, and Washington, after a gallant struggle, had to capitulate.

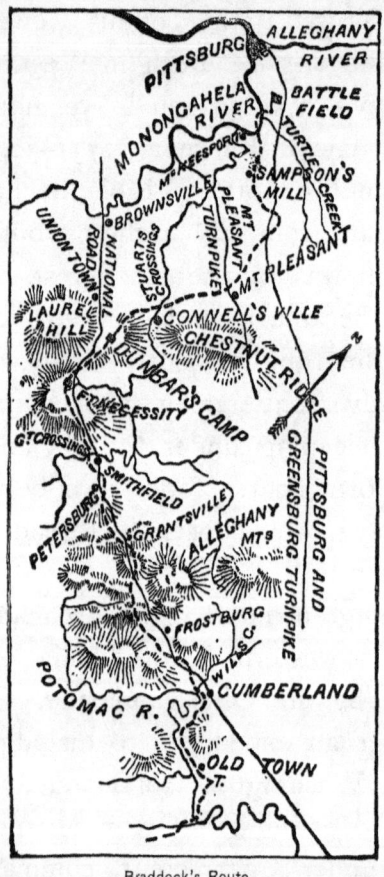

Braddock's Route.

This was on July 3, 1754. The French and Indian War had begun.

The English Government bade the colonies defend their frontier, and in this interest twenty-five delegates from the seven northern colonies met at Albany on June 19, 1754. Benjamin Franklin represented Pennsylvania, and it was at this conference that he presented his well-considered plan, to be described in our chapter on Independence, for a general government over English America. The Albany Convention amounted to little, but did somewhat to renew alliance with the Six Nations.[1]

In this decisive war England had in view four great objects of conquest in America: 1. Fort Du Quesne; 2. The Ontario basin with Oswego and Fort Niagara; 3. The Champlain Valley; 4. Louisburg. The British ministry seemed in earnest. It sent Sir Edward Braddock to this side with six thousand splendidly equipped veterans, and offered large sums for fitting out regiments of provincials. Braddock arrived in February, 1755, but moved very languidly. This was not altogether his fault, for he

[1] Increased from five to six by the accession of the Tuscaroras.

had difficulties with the governors and they with their legislatures.

At last off for Fort Du Quesne, he took a needlessly long route, through Virginia instead of Pennsylvania. He scorned ad-

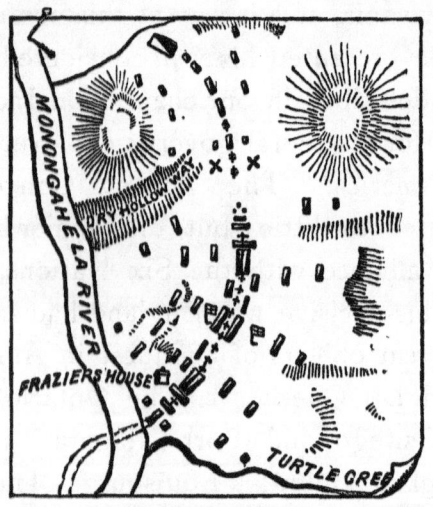

Map of Braddock's Field.

vice, marching and fighting stiffly according to the rules of the Old World military art, heeding none of Franklin's and Washington's sage hints touching savage modes of warfare. The consequence was this brave Briton's defeat and death. As he drew near to Fort Du Quesne, he fell into a care-

The Death of Braddock.

fully prepared ambuscade. Four horses were shot under him. Mounting a fifth he spurred to the front to inspire his men, forbidding them seek the slightest cover, as Washington urged and as the provincials successfully did. The regulars, obeying, were half of them killed in their tracks, the remainder retreating, in panic at first, to Philadelphia. Braddock died, and was buried at Great Meadows, where his grave is still to be seen.

Washington was the only mounted officer in this action who was not killed or fatally wounded, a fact at the time regarded specially providential. On his return, aged twenty-three, the Rev. Samuel Davies, afterward President of the College of New Jersey, referred to him in his sermon as "that heroic youth, Colonel Washington, whom I cannot but hope Providence has preserved in so signal a manner for some important service to his country."

The early part of this war witnessed the tragic occurrence immortalized by Longfellow's "Evangeline," the expulsion of the

French from Acadia. The poem is too favorable to these people. They had never become reconciled to English rule, and were believed on strong evidence to be active in promoting French schemes against the English. It was resolved to scatter them among the Atlantic settlements. The act was savage, and became doubly so through the unmeant cruelties attending its execution. The poor wretches were huddled on the shore weeks too soon for their transports. Families were broken up, children forcibly separated from parents. The largest company was carried to Massachusetts, many to Pennsylvania, some to the extreme South. Not a few, crushed in spirit, became paupers. A number found their way to France, a number to Louisiana, a handful back to Nova Scotia.

Braddock was succeeded by the fussy and incompetent Earl of Loudon, 1756-57, whom Franklin likened to Saint George on the sign-posts, "always galloping but never advancing." He gathered twelve thousand men for the recapture of Lou-

[1757] *THE FRENCH AND INDIAN WAR* 361

isburg, but exaggerated reports of the French strength frightened him from the attempt. Similar inaction lost him Fort

Montcalm.

William Henry on Lake George. The end of the year 1757 saw the English cause on this side at low ebb, Montcalm, the tried and brilliant French commander, having outwitted or frightened the English officers at every point.

From this moment all changes. William Pitt, subsequently Lord Chatham, now became the soul of the British ministry.

William Pitt.

George III. had dismissed him therefrom in 1757, but Newcastle found it impossible to get on without him. The great commoner had to be recalled, this time to take entire direction of the war.

Pitt had set his mind on the conquest of Canada. He superseded Loudon early in 1758 by General Amherst, who was seconded by Wolfe and by Admiral Boscawen, both with large re-enforcements. They were to reduce Louisburg. It was an innovation to assign important commands like these to men with so little fame and influence, but Pitt did not care. He believed his appointees to be brave, energetic, skilful, and the event proved his wisdom. Louisburg fell, and with it the whole of Cape Breton Island and also Prince Edward.

Unfortunately General Abercrombie had not been recalled with Loudon. The same year, 1758, he signally failed to capture Ticonderoga, leaving the way to Montreal worse blocked than before. Fort Du Quesne, however, General Forbes took this year at little cost, rechristening it Pittsburgh in honor of the heroic minister who had ordered the enterprise.

In the year 1759 occurred a grand triple

movement upon Canada. Amherst, now general-in-chief, was to clear the Champlain

General Wolfe.

Valley, and Prideaux with large colonial forces to reduce Fort Niagara. Both had orders, being successful in these initial attacks, to move down the St. Lawrence and unite with Wolfe, who was to sail up that river and beset Quebec. Prideaux was splendidly successful, as indeed was Amherst in time, though longer than he anticipated in securing Ticonderoga and Crown Point.

Meantime Wolfe at Quebec was trying in all ways to manœuvre the crafty Montcalm out of his impregnable works. Failing, he in his eagerness suffered himself to attempt an assault upon the city, which proved not only vain but terribly costly. A weaker commander would now have given up, but Wolfe had red hair, and the grit usually accompanying. Undaunted, he planned the hazardous enterprise of rowing up the St. Lawrence by night, landing with five thousand picked men at the foot of the precipitous ascent to the Plains of Abraham, and scaling those heights to face Montcalm from the west. The Frenchman, stunned at the sight which day brought him, lost no time in attacking. In the hot battle which ensued, September 13, 1759, both commanders fell, Wolfe cheering his heroes to sure victory, Montcalm urging on his forlorn hope in vain. The English remained masters of the field and in five days Quebec capitulated.

Vaudreuil, the French

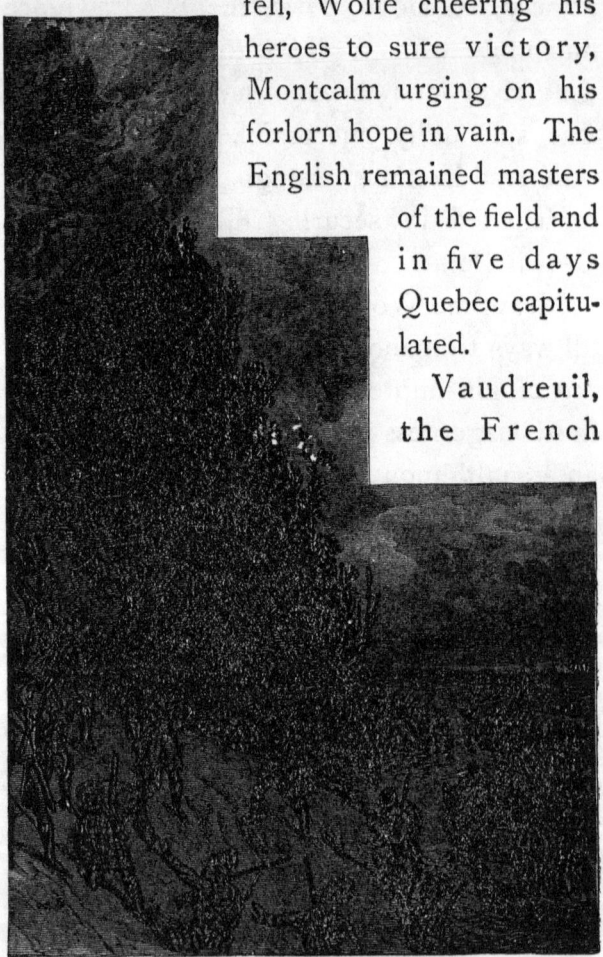

Landing of Wolfe.

commander at Montreal, sought to dislodge
the English ere the ice left the river in the

Quebec in 1730—From an old Print.

spring of 1760, and succeeded in driving
them within their works. Each side then
waited and hoped for help from beyond sea

so soon as navigation opened. It came the earlier to the English, who were gladdened on May 11th by the approach of a British frigate, the forerunner of a fleet. They now chased Vaudreuil back into Montreal, where they were met by Haviland from Crown Point and by Amherst from Oswego. France's days of power in America were ended. Her fleet of twenty-two sail intended for succor met total destruction in the Bay des Chaleurs, and by the Peace of Paris, 1763, she surrendered to her victorious antagonist every foot of her American territory east of the Mississippi, save the city of New Orleans.

The Indians were thus left to finish this war alone. Pontiac, the brave and cunning chief of the Ottawas, aghast at the rising might of the English, and the certain fate of his race without the French for helpers, organized a conspiracy including nearly every tribe this side the Mississippi except the Six Nations, to put to the sword all the English garrisons in the West. Fatal success waited upon the plan. It was in 1763.

1763] THE FRENCH AND INDIAN WAR 369

Forts Sandusky, St. Joseph (southeast of Lake Michigan), Miami (Fort Wayne), Presque Isle (Erie, Pa.), Le Bœuf, Venango, and Pittsburgh were attacked and

Bouquet's Redoubt at Pittsburgh.

all but the last destroyed, soldiers and settlers murdered with indescribable barbarities. Pittsburgh held out till re-enforced, at dreadful cost in blood, by Colonel Bouquet and his Highlanders, who marched from Philadelphia.

The hottest and longest conflict was at Detroit, Major Gladwyn commanding, where Pontiac himself led the onset, heading perhaps a thousand men. The siege was maintained with fearful venom from May 11th till into October. The English tried a number of sallies, brave, fatal, vain, and were so hard pressed by their bloodthirsty foe that only timely and repeated re-enforcements saved them. At last the savages, becoming, as always, disunited and straitened for supplies, sullenly made peace; and at the call of the rich and now free Northwest, caravans of English immigrants thronged thither to lay under happiest auspices the foundations of new States.

END OF VOLUME I.

www.ingramcontent.com/pod-product-compliance
Lightning Source LLC
Chambersburg PA
CBHW020635230426
43665CB00008B/177